For Jacques—

who was there
at the beginning—
and the end—
with esteem

[signature]

Jan. 63

Kennedy
A TIME REMEMBERED

Kennedy
A TIME REMEMBERED

JACQUES LOWE

A Quartet/Visual Arts Book

Other books by Jacques Lowe
Quartet/Visual Arts
The City
The Incredible Music Machine
Queen's Greatest Pix

Others
Kentucky. A Celebration of American Life
Celebration at Persepolis
Pilgrimage
The Kennedy Years
Portrait. The Emergence of John F. Kennedy

A Quartet/Visual Arts Book
First published in 1983
Simultaneously in the UK by Quartet Books Limited
27/29 Goodge Street, London W1P 1FD
and in the USA by Quartet Books Inc.
360 Park Avenue South, New York NY 10010

Copyright © Jacques Lowe & Visual Arts LG SA 1983

Printed in Italy by Sagdos, Brugherio

Acknowledgments for material quoted in this book appear
at the end of the book.

British Library Cataloguing in Publication Data

Lowe, Jacques
    Kennedy, a time remembered.
    1. Kennedy (*Family*) — Biography.
    I. Title
    973.92'092'2   E843
    ISBN 0-7043-2404-0

Library of Congress Cataloging in Publication Data

Lowe, Jacques
    Kennedy, a time remembered.

    (A Quartet/Visual Arts Book)
    Includes index.
    1. Kennedy, John F. (John Fitzgerald), 1917–1963 —
Iconography. 2. Presidents — United States — Iconography.
I. Title.
E842.1.L65 1983   973.922'092'4   (B)   83-10985
ISBN 0-7043-2404-0

This book is dedicated to the spirit of a truly remarkable family and to America, a nation of immigrants, who include the author.
Jacques Lowe

. . .

Has anybody here
Seen my old friend John?
Can you tell me
Where he's gone?
He freed a lot of people
But it seems
The good die young
I just looked around
And he was gone

Has anybody here
Seen my old friend Martin?
Can you tell me
Where he's gone?
He freed a lot of people
But it seems
The good die young
I just looked around
And he was gone

Has anybody here
Seen my old friend Bobby?
Can you tell me
Where he's gone?
He freed a lot of people
But it seems
The good die young
I just looked around
And he was gone

Oh I just looked around
And they were gone

Abraham, Martin and John
Words and music by Dick Holler,
recorded by Dion and Marvin Gaye

HUMBLE BEGINNINGS

The First Generation

MAYOR JOHN F. FITZGERALD
OF BOSTON
AND FAMILY—
OLD HOME WEEK 1907

A 1907 portrait of John F. "Honey Fitz" Fitzgerald and family. His wife, Mary Hannon Fitzgerald, is on the left, with her arm around their son Frederick. Other children (left to right): Eunice and Agnes, Tom and John F. Jr., and Rose, mother of the future President. Honey Fitz's father, Thomas, had come to Boston from County Wexford in Ireland, during the potato famine of 1840, one of a group of penniless, desperate men and women, for whom survival in the new land meant poverty, tenements and endless hours of backbreaking labour. Rose Mary Murray had also made that journey from Ireland and married Thomas in Boston, where they met. But both died in their thirties, leaving nine children behind and little money.

Honey Fitz, third in line, had to leave Harvard Medical School, where he had been accepted after promising years at Boston Latin School, in order to help care for the brothers and sisters left behind.

He and the family survived and he soon entered ward politics, one of the few professions left open to the Irish in a city dominated by the "Boston Brahmins". By 1895 he had run successfully for Congress, serving three terms, and by 1906 he had been elected Mayor of Boston, a tenure which preserved his fame. His political bailiwick was The North End, the place where young Jack Kennedy was to start his rise to the White House, and, an insufferable extrovert, he had attended every wedding, wake and Holy Communion, singing his famous "campaign" ditty "Sweet Adeline", often standing on a table.

8

Sweet A-del-ine, My A-del-ine,
At night, dear heart, For you I pine;
In all my dreams, Your fair face beams,
You're the flower of my heart,
Sweet Adeline.

Words and music by Richard H. Gerard and Harry Armstrong

"I have played it a few thousand times."

ROSE FITZGERALD

THE NOTMAN PHOTOGRAPHIC C? LIMITED — 3 PARK ST. BOSTON

Above, right: Patrick J. Kennedy, whose father, Patrick, also came from Wexford during the famine, married Bridget Murphy, had four children and died penniless at thirty-five. Patrick Joseph, the youngest, helped his mother around the small "notions" store she managed with difficulty, took odd jobs around the waterfront and, when strong enough, became a stevedore, then and now one of the toughest and hardest labourer's jobs available. Because of the family's impoverished state, he never finished grade school.

But young P.J., as he became known in later political life, had a head for business. Starting with a neighbourhood bar on scrimped savings, he soon expanded his small empire into partnerships with other bars, or "saloons" as they were known in the Irish neighbourhoods; went into the coal business, the wholesale liquor business and finally into banking. By the time Joseph P. Kennedy, the President's father, was born, P.J. was a success.

He had married Mary Hickey, daughter of a "substantial" family, and become a political force in Boston's East End. Unlike Honey Fitz, P.J. preferred working behind the scenes to running for office, which, however, he had also done successfully, and his awesome power and control over his part of the city was concentrated in the "Board of Strategy", the group which selected candidates for political office.

Right: Mary Hickey Kennedy with Joseph P. "Joe" and his sister Johanna at Old Orchard Beach, Maine, in 1894.

Fourth of July in Concord, Mass. Honey Fitz near flagpole.

"I am the first son of foreign parents to become Mayor of Boston, thus my parents were the first persons of immigrant stock to have a son a mayor."
JOHN F. FITZGERALD

"Grandfather Fitzgerald was Mayor of Boston and a congressman and then my grandfather Kennedy was a political leader of East Boston, although they didn't get along well. They lived and operated and worked at the same time. My grandfather Kennedy operated at a tavern in East Boston, but he was terribly straight-laced and he sometimes disapproved of my grandfather Fitzgerald."
ROBERT F. KENNEDY

Top: Vice President Fairbanks, Josiah P. Quincy and Honey Fitz on July 31, 1907.

Centre: Old Home Week, Boston, July 29, 1907. Honey Fitz is flanked by B. L. School and Edward Everett Hale on his right.

Right: Dorchester Day, June 8, 1907.

Old Orchard Beach, Maine, was the summer retreat for both the Fitzgeralds and the Kennedys, along with most of Boston's Irish politicians. Rose first met Joe there, but they didn't really speak. Second from left is P. J. Kennedy, then Rose Fitzgerald and Honey Fitz. Second from right is Joe Kennedy.

Honey Fitz can talk you blind
On any subject you can find.
Fish and fishing, motorboats,
Railroads, streetcars, getting votes,
Proper ways to open clams,
How to cure existing shams;
State Street, Goo-Goos, aeroplanes,
Malefactors, thieving gains,
Local transportation rates,
How to run the nearby states;
On all these things, and many more,
Honey Fitz is crammed with lore.

From a Boston newspaper

Honey Fitz at Old Orchard Beach with a friend in boater hats.

During a time when the "Help Wanted" ads specified
"No Irish Need Apply", Honey Fitz continued to
dominate Irish politics, entertaining in grand
style the likes of Sir Thomas Lipton, the tea
magnate, and Admiral Togo of Japan. Joe and
Rose now began to "go steady".

June 1911

Rose in Panama. *Below:* Rose, Agnes, Honey Fitz and Eunice in Boston Harbor.

"I remember that as we walked through Phoenix Park in Dublin, laced with paths and full of flowers, my father pointed out the place where a member of the underground Irish republican army had assassinated the British Chief Secretary for Ireland, Lord Frederick Charles Cavendish on May 6, 1882. Among many things I could not have imagined was that someday I would have a daughter, Kathleen, who would marry Lord Cavendish's grandnephew, Billy Hartington."

ROSE FITZGERALD

"I grew up with the idea that one should be careful with money, that none should be spent without good and sufficient reason — tangible or intangible — to justify each expense."

ROSE FITZGERALD

Rose in 1911 wearing one of the big hats she liked so much and finally had made to order.

The upwardly mobile Irish in Boston were called Lace Curtain Irish, which some said meant ''a family that has fruit in the house when nobody is sick''. Rose's ''debut'' was the epitome of that social class.

"Though it was the dead of winter, my parents had turned the house into a bower of roses for me . . . I wore a white satin dress with a short train; the bodice and skirt were embroidered in white, with just a touch of yellow silk ribbon showing through the embroidery along the hemline . . . with my mother in black Chantilly lace and my father in cutaway and winged collar, I received the guests in the drawing room. I was so excited by the occasion that I felt no fatigue standing three or four hours and shaking hands and chatting with more than 450 people, among them the new governor, two congressmen and numerous other dignitaries . . ."
ROSE FITZGERALD

"Who makes the laws of the Nation?"
"John F. Fitzgerald."
"Who is the President of the United States?"
"John F. Fitzgerald."

Irish immigrant in Boston during Honey Fitz's time as Mayor, as told by James M. Curley, a political rival

Rose, because of her mother's reluctance to leave the hearth, became her father's official companion, hostess and assistant on his travels, whether political or in aid of Boston's Chamber of Commerce, which included trips to Hamburg and the newly built Panama Canal to gauge the effects of these ports on the well-being of "A Bigger, Better, Busier Boston". In 1908 they set out on a trip that was to take them to Ireland, England, Belgium, France, Switzerland, Germany and Holland.

Rose and her father in Ireland.

Honey Fitz, Rose and friends in Germany.

"It seems to me that boys in those days were a little more enterprising than they are now. What fifteen-year-old boy would hire a ball-park today?"
JOSEPH P. KENNEDY

The Assumptions neighbourhood baseball team with Joe Kennedy second from the upper right. Joe had raised the money to outfit the team in white uniforms sporting the letter A, blue stockings and spiked shoes. After seeing the team attract a reasonable number of spectators, he hired a park and sold tickets to the games, ending up with a profit. He was fifteen years old.

"During the last year at Dorchester High and the following year . . . Joe and I managed to see each other rather often. Less often than we would have liked, but more often than my father was aware of, and enough in any case to reaffirm in our hearts how deeply we cared for each other . . . I suppose no father really thinks any man is good enough for his daughter. But my father was a hopeless case . . . believing that I could take my pick of any beau . . . he didn't want me . . . pledging my heart prematurely to any young man, however attractive and brilliant he might be."

ROSE FITZGERALD KENNEDY

"We went steady for seven years before we were married . . . but I was never seriously interested in anyone else."

JOSEPH P. KENNEDY

Rose Fitzgerald and Joseph P. Kennedy married in October of 1914. The courtship was first opposed by Rose's father, who had arranged trips to Palm Beach, Florida and even to Europe and Central America to break up the romance. But Rose was determined. Honey Fitz consented and never regretted it.

A CLAN TO BE RECKONED WITH

Joseph P. Kennedy and the Rise of an Irish Aristocracy

"Second best is a loser."
JOSEPH P. KENNEDY

John F. Kennedy aged one, Nantucket, Mass.

"As a baby, Jack had a little difficulty with his infant feeding, and then he had scarlet fever when he was only four years old, and I think that did affect his childhood a bit.

"One day I took them out on a blueberry party. There were about five of us, including Jack, but Eunice was stung by a bumblebee, and that made everyone else rather nervous, and after I'd quieted her down, Jack sat in an ant hill, so he had ants all over him for a few minutes. I became rather discouraged and packed them all into the station wagon and bought some blueberries at the neighborhood store."
ROSE KENNEDY

Rose Kennedy with Joe Jr. (left), Rosemary and Jack.

*"Whenever I held my newborn babe in my arms, I used to think
what I did and what I said to him would have an influence, not only on
him, but on all whom he met, not for a day, a month, or a year, but for
time and for eternity."*

ROSE KENNEDY from *Rose*, a film produced by the Kennedy family

The couple iceskating in Poland Springs, Maine, December 1914.

Joseph P. with Joe Jr. and Jack, Brookline, Mass. 1919. Jack is two years old.

"I have a strong idea that there is no other success for a father and a mother except to feel that they have made some contribution to the development of their children."
JOSEPH P. KENNEDY

The brothers in 1921.

"In a family, all the children are different . . . Bring up the oldest ones the way you want them all to go. If the oldest ones come in and say good night to their parents or say their prayers in the morning, the younger ones think that's probably a good thing to do, and they will do it."
ROSE KENNEDY

Jack, Rosemary, Kathleen and Eunice with their father at Hyannis Port, Mass. in 1925.

"Exercise discipline, as well as love, provide limits, as well
as freedom. I taught them to reach for the outer edge of
their endowments — bracket the children's activities to
the rhythm of the seasons — to the strength of the wind,
the salt of the sea, and the excitement of the snow."
ROSE KENNEDY

Jack and Rosemary (top left) and Joe Jr., Kathleen, Rosemary and Jack (top right) during summer vacations in 1923 in Cohasset, Mass. Cohasset again (centre left and right and bottom left) in 1924 and finally Joe Jr., cousin Ann Gargan and Jack at Hyannis Port in 1925, where they were to summer for the rest of their lives.

Rosemary, Jack, little Eunice, Joe Jr. and Kathleen in Hyannis Port.

Joe Jr. and Jack in front of the house in Hyannis Port, 1925.

"When Jack was a little fellow, we used to go bathing two or three miles from here at a beach club. The children were all supposed to be ready to go home at one o'clock. Jack was invariably late, so we would get into the car and drive off home without him. We would start lunch, and the rule was that if someone was late for lunch, he would just be served the course or second vegetable which was being served at that moment; he couldn't start from the beginning. Jack would arrive in somebody else's car, perfectly happy, and then after lunch he would go in the kitchen, and the cook would give him everything he wanted to eat. I knew this was going on. Perhaps it was poor discipline, but he was apt to be rather thin, and I didn't think it was too serious a habit, so I used to let it go.

"One day when the boys were sitting at a little table in the dining room and Mr. Kennedy and I were at the big table, they were having their lunch, and they had cake with chocolate frosting. Joe took his chocolate frosting off to save it till the end. Just before the end of the meal, Jack reached over, took it and put it in his mouth before anybody could say yes or no. Of course Joe immediately got up and gave him a good whack."

ROSE KENNEDY

Young Jack as a Keystone cop. Brookline, Mass. 1925.

"A PLEA FOR A RAISE"
By Jack Kennedy
Dedicated to my Mr. J.P. Kennedy

Chapter 1

My recent allowance is 40¢. This I used for aeroplanes and other playthings of childhood but now I am a scout and I put away my childish things. Before I would spend 20¢ of my 40¢ allowance and in five minutes I would have empty pockets and nothing to gain and 20¢ to lose. When I am a scout I have to buy canteens, haversacks, blankets, searchlights, poncho, things that will last for years and I can always use it while I can't use a chocolate marshmallow sundae with vanilla ice cream and so I put in my plea for a raise of thirty cents for me to buy scout things and pay my own way more around.

Finis
John Fitzgerald Francis Kennedy

Skiing in Poland Springs, Maine 1925.

Joe Jr. (left) and Jack at Hyannis Port, 1925.

Jack (centre) and Joe Jr. (right) with a friend in Brookline in 1923.

Brookline, summer 1924. From left, Kathleen, a friend, Eunice, Jack and Rosemary.

Rose Kennedy, Sir Thomas Lipton and Rose Kennedy's sisters Agnes and Eunice on a boat trip in Massachusetts. Sir Thomas was a friend of Rose's father, Honey Fitz, and at one time was rumoured to be her suitor.

"We stopped off in England for a few days and were at Cowes at the time of one of the great boating regattas. My father had earlier become a warm friend of Sir Thomas Lipton, the famous merchant and yachtsman, who used to bring his ocean racers to our waters to race for the America's Cup. We had entertained him in Boston . . . We had already been aboard his big seagoing residential yacht Erin several times . . . and, as my father related the story: 'Rose sighted Lipton's Erin in the distance and we went down to a wharf, hoping to find a motorboat that could take us out . . . we noticed the King's launch and thought one of the members of the royal family was aboard. The launch came up to the wharf . . . the officer in charge came up to where I was and asked if he could be of any service . . . I told him I was a friend of Sir Thomas and was looking for a boat to carry us to the Erin. The officer graciously said the King's launch was at my service.

Joseph P. Kennedy Sr. and his wife on a California beach in 1927. The elder Kennedy was deeply involved in the movie business at that time.

" 'As we approached the Erin Sir Thomas saw us through his glass, and figuring it was some member of the royal party, possibly the King or Queen, he had all his crew brought forward on the deck to receive these eminent guests. Among his guests were some Americans, and they were all anxiously asking Sir Thomas as to the etiquette to be followed immediately upon the approach of the King or Queen. Sir Thomas was busily explaining when the boat arrived and as I popped my head over the rail he nearly fell on the deck, so great was his surprise. "My heavens," he said, "it's my friend, John Fitzgerald of Boston, with Rose and Agnes." . . . Apparently, there was a small crisis when the King and Queen arrived to find their launch gone and "nowhere to be seen" while they were "waiting impatiently on the jetty". But there was a happy ending. Sir Thomas explained everything. King Edward VII was not irritated but amused.' "

ROSE KENNEDY

Joe Jr., Joseph P. Kennedy and Jack in Palm Beach, 1931.

The country was still struggling to free itself from the severe economic depression, but Joe Kennedy Sr. was secure. He had been one of the legendary speculators on the wildest stock market in history, that of the 1920s, but he had come out intact, selling long before the crash. He had set up a Million Dollar Trust Fund for each of his children, so ''they could spit me in the eye if they wished''. He had been a noted trouble-shooter for major business corporations, at one time spending seven weeks in a hotel room, sick with neuritis, and from his sickbed in New York, saving John Hertz's Yellow Cab Company from collapse.

He had bought a chain of New England movie houses, taken over Film Booking Offices of America and put that company back in the black by producing low-cost westerns at the rate of one a week. He became Chairman of Pathé and gained control of the Keith Albee Orpheum circuit, a major film distribution organization. He had achieved some notoriety by producing *Queen Kelly*, starring Gloria Swanson, with whom he was thought to be romantically involved. On that picture he had hired and then fired Erich von Stroheim and eventually had to scrap the picture at a loss of one million dollars, a fortune for those times. But by the end of the 1920s he had quit Hollywood for good, five million dollars ahead.

The early 1930s saw him moving into real estate, eventually buying the Merchandise Mart in Chicago, then the largest building in the country after the Empire State building, as well as a liquor importing business. He continued to prosper.

But the depression, although he was not personally hurt, made a deep impression on him. His faith in the ultimate security of the economic system was shaken and he felt that radical changes were necessary to correct the faults. He became an ardent backer of Franklin Roosevelt's campaign for the presidency and after Roosevelt's election Kennedy accepted the position as the first Chairman of the Securities & Exchange Commission, the regulatory agency that was to change Wall Street from a gambling mart into a federally supervised, responsible body of investment houses.

Kennedy's appointment and his fame as one of the most notorious manipulators in the very market he was to regulate caused loud protests from reformers and conservatives alike. Yet Kennedy's chairmanship of the commission was highly effective and within a year both factions hailed his achievements. He had also made a permanent friend in the White House, which was to pay big dividends later.

Bobby and Teddy with "Kikoo", their governess, in a rickshaw-like straw chair on wheels, a typical Palm Beach vehicle in those days.

Right, top to bottom: The summer of 1934, Palm Beach. The youngest children are here with Kikoo. From the left, Jean, Teddy, Pat and Bobby Kennedy.

Bobby (left) entering a prize fight at the Sea Spray Club in Palm Beach, 1935.

Betsy Roosevelt and Eunice sit on the edge of the Palm Beach swimming pool. In the water are Jean, Pat and Bobby.

Exercise classes on the beach. Teddy and Jean on the right, with friends, Bobby watching. Note the lack of co-ordination of these children, who were later to become athletes.

Top: Hyannis Port, 1927. *Above:* Jack Kennedy at Choate School in 1934–5 with his friends known as the "Muckers Club". Second from the left is Jack's life-long friend LeMoyne "Lem" Billings. Jack was to graduate that year from Choate having no career plans whatsoever, and he came out sixty-fourth in a class of 112. Still, his classmates voted him "most likely to succeed".

"The time came when we had to tell the children that their father was well to do. We were careful to emphasize that money brought responsibility. I used to quote from St. Luke to the children, 'To whom much has been given, much will be required.' When great blessings are received, large obligations are owed."
ROSE KENNEDY, from the film *Rose*

"Jack took the New York Times at Choate. I don't think... any other kid... subscribed to the New York Times at fourteen, fifteen, and read it every morning."
LEMOYNE BILLINGS

"At Hyannis Port, in what used to be part of the basement, we installed a little theater... It had a little stage for the children's theatrical productions, but primarily it was a movie theater. Because of Joe's position in the industry he was able to borrow practically any film... which gave us an inexhaustible supply of home entertainment ... Consequently our summers at Hyannis Port took on something of the character of a modern movie festival, with a different film being shown three or four evenings a week."
ROSE KENNEDY

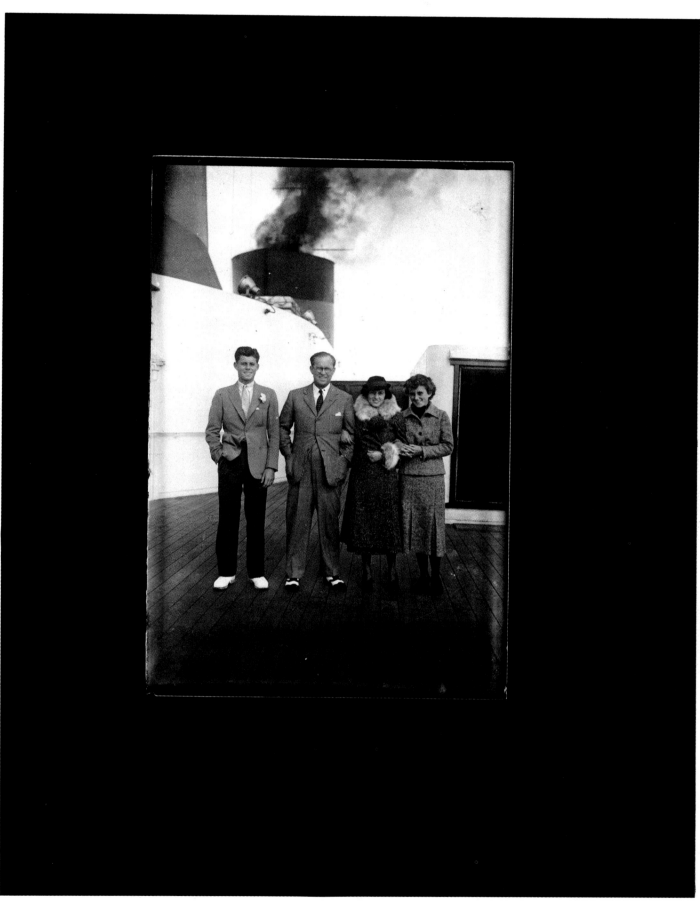

The family en route to Europe in the summer of 1935. From left, Jack, his father, his mother and his sister Kathleen.

Palm Beach, 1935. Pat with a friend in the foreground, Lem Billings, Bobby and Jack standing.

"Bobby had a paper route. That pleased us, of course. The 'paper boy' is practically an American symbol of boyhood spunk and ambition. Then . . . I found out he had talked the chauffeur into driving him. There he was, riding around all over Bronxville — making his deliveries from a Rolls-Royce. Needless to say I put a stop to this at once."

ROSE KENNEDY

Bobby in foreground. Jack carrying Teddy on his shoulders.
Right, top to bottom: Teddy, Jack and Bobby in 1936.
Bobby and Pat in Bronxville.
Bobby, Jean and Eunice in Bronxville, 1935.
Young Teddy, with a friend, steering his own boat.

Kathleen, Rosemary and Rose Kennedy getting ready for the presentation at the Court of St. James on May 11, 1938.

"I started school today. This was the season for cricket. I didn't do too well. We had decimals in maths class, I played fives at break and before lunch a little bit. I went to confession at church and then came home and had a light supper because tonight was the night the King and Queen were coming to the embassy. Just before the King and Queen arrived we went in with all the guests. The Queen said that Jack and I were the only two she hadn't yet met. The King and Queen were wonderful."

YOUNG BOBBY KENNEDY

King George VI and Queen Elizabeth met by Ambassador Joseph P. Kennedy on their arrival at Victoria station from their trip to the United States, May 1939.

In 1937 President Roosevelt appointed Joseph P. Kennedy Ambassador to the Court of St. James. Kennedy had successfully completed a second Roosevelt assignment, the reorganization of the Maritime Commission, and Roosevelt had written, "Dear Joe. You have maintained your justly earned reputation of being a two-fisted, hard-hitting executive," but again "all hell broke loose" following the appointment. Here was the most crucial diplomatic post, especially at a time when Hitler was growing stronger and more threatening every day, and it was going not only to a non-career foreign service officer, but to an Irish Catholic, a hot-tempered, blunt and outspoken one to boot. At first sight, hardly an ideal choice. But the wily President, concerned with trade and England's war debt and feeling the need for a financial man in the post, persevered and the conservative Secretary of State, Cordell Hull (who met Kennedy only after the appointment), and his department acquiesced.

But the new American Ambassador, his beautiful wife and their nine children were an instant success in London. Playing golf shortly after his arrival and making a hole in one, his statement, "I am much happier being the father of nine children and making a hole in one than I would be as the father of one child making a hole in nine," made him the delight of Fleet Street, which from then on reported his every movement and utterance, including the length of trousers he wore at official receptions.

By 1938 Ambassador Kennedy had also become a close friend of Tory Prime Minister Neville Chamberlain. They agreed that having given in to Hitler on Czechoslovakia had assured "Peace in Our Time", an opinion which was anathema to the President and *his* British friend, Winston Churchill. At a speech to the British Navy League Kennedy asserted that the world was big enough to accommodate both democracies and dictatorships, and he came up with a plan to rescue Germany's 600,000 Jews by resettling them in British colonies and sparsely populated areas of the world. *LIFE* wrote the following week: "Kennedy is rated the most influential Ambassador in England for many years. If his plan for settling the German Jews, already widely known as the 'Kennedy Plan', succeeds, it will add new luster to a reputation which may well carry Joseph Patrick Kennedy into the White House." This was a prospect not dear to the incumbent President.

By 1940 events had overtaken the Ambassador. The war had begun, Winston Churchill was in office and Roosevelt was fully backing the British war effort. Kennedy, having pleaded not to supply Britain with armaments and given one more disastrous interview to the *Boston Globe,* in which he said: "There's no sense in our getting in. We'd only be holding the bag . . . Democracy is finished in England . . .", finally handed in his resignation, which was speedily accepted.

"If John Kennedy is characteristic of the new generation . . . many of us would be happy to have the destinies of this republic handed over to this generation at once."

HENRY R. LUCE, in his foreword to *Why England Slept*

By 1938 Jack was a sophomore at Harvard and he had begun travelling widely in Europe. He asked penetrating questions of all he met, checked the answers, probed, and reported the results to his father in London. Jack became fascinated with the entire spectrum of European politics, and especially England's role. On graduation in 1940 his honour thesis in political science was based on these observations. Entitled *Why England Slept,* the paper was published and became an instant bestseller. Europe was being overrun by the Nazis and the timely book made the young author, barely twenty-three, an instant celebrity. But soon, he and his older brother would join the war effort, Joe Jr. never to return. And their father, who had so strenuously resisted America's entry into the war, would lose both his favourite son and his son-in-law.

"Two things I always knew about you. One that you are smart and two that you are a swell guy. Love, Dad."

JOSEPH P. KENNEDY, in a telegram congratulating Jack on his cum laude graduation from Harvard and magna cum laude grade on his thesis in political science

Top to bottom: Jack Kennedy dancing at the American Embassy in London; Skiing instruction in St. Moritz, winter 1938. From left, Pat, Eunice, Bobby, Joe Jr. and Rosemary; The family at Eden Roc in Cannes, July 1939.

"It is true that the democratic and dictator countries have important and fundamental divergencies of outlook, which in certain matters go deeper than politics. But there is simply no sense . . . in letting these differences grow into unrelenting antagonisms. After all, we have to live together in the same world, whether we like it or not."

JOSEPH P. KENNEDY, British Navy League speech

"One has . . . to give credit to Joe Kennedy that he was sitting right there with the bombs . . . there was no lack of being on the job . . . but most notably, in 1940, he thought that England was sure to be beaten. He put this in most colorful language . . . from the point of view of objective calculation, he couldn't be faulted. The odds were considerably against Britain at the time."

HENRY R. LUCE

"This is not our war, we were not consulted when it began, we have no veto power over its continuance."

JOSEPH P. KENNEDY

Again in St. Moritz in a horsedrawn sled. Eunice, Bobby, Rosemary and Jean, Rose and Teddy.

"To say that democracy has been awakened by the events of the last few weeks is not enough. Any person will awaken when the house is burning down. What we need is an armed guard that will wake when the fire first starts, or, better yet, one that will not permit the fire to start at all . . . We should profit by the lesson of England and make our democracy work . . . Any system of government will work when everything is going well. It is the system that functions in the pinches that survives."

JOHN F. KENNEDY, *Why England Slept*

While Joseph P. Kennedy was United States Ambassador to Great Britain, the family was photographed at the US Embassy by society photographer Marcus Adams. From left to right, Rose Kennedy, wearing a tiara, Teddy, Rosemary, Joe Jr., Ambassador Kennedy, Eunice, Jean, Jack, Bobby, Patricia and Kathleen. The ensemble is truly ''royal''

Following page, left, top to bottom: Kathleen and Jack; Jack and friends; Jack, grandfather Honey Fitz and Joe Jr.; Palm Beach. *Right, top:* Edgartown Regatta. *Right, bottom:* Kathleen, now Lady Hartington, in 1944 in England. Kathleen ''Kick'' had married William John Robert Cavendish, ''Billy'', Marquess of Hartington, and future Duke of Devonshire that year. Her older brother Joe Jr. was best man. Both officers, they wore their uniforms at the wedding, that of the Coldstream Guards, and that of a US Navy flier. Both were to be killed in action within four months of the wedding.

The last year to re-unite the family was 1944. It was after John F. Kennedy's Pacific war experience (later) and his comrades-in-arms from PT 109 Jim Reed and Len Thom and their wives, as well as Barney Ross and Red Fay joined the Kennedys in Hyannis Port.

"I was fascinated by them. Jack was autographing copies of Why England Slept *while Grandfather Fitzgerald was reading to him a political story from a newspaper. Young Joe was telling about something that happened to him in Russia. Mrs. Kennedy was talking on the phone with Cardinal Spellman. A tall and very attractive girl in a sweat shirt and dungarees, who turned out to be Pat, was describing how a German Messerschmitt plane had crashed near her father's house outside of London. Bobby was trying to get everybody to play charades. The next thing I knew, all of us were choosing up sides for touch football, and Kathleen was calling the plays in the huddle for the team I was on. There was something doing every minute."*

CHARLES SPAULDING, later to become Jack Kennedy's close friend, on first meeting the Kennedys in 1940

WAR, POLITICS AND FAMILY

Hero, Congressman, Senator, Husband and Father

By the end of 1941, both brothers had been accepted by the Navy. Jack Kennedy had been rejected at first by both the Army and the Navy because of a football injury to his back, but for five months he had undertaken special exercises to strengthen his back, and, on reapplication, he was allowed to join. The two proud brothers, both to become war heroes, had themselves photographed in a jovial mood.

Early in 1943, Jack Kennedy's repeated requests to be assigned combat duty, aided by some string-pulling, were finally granted. He was shipped out to the South Pacific and given command of PT 109, a torpedo boat. Operating off Tulagi and the Russell Islands, he was a cog in a vast sea—air offensive against the Japanese around New Georgia, Solomon Islands.

Jack's last home leave. Left, Torbert MacDonald, a Harvard room-mate, who had also joined the Navy after Pearl Harbor, leaving his law studies in mid-term. Patriotism was rampant and the young men were raring to go.

"In August of 1943, we faced death in the Solomon Islands. That any of us survived is a tribute to the man who was our commanding officer, Lt. John F. Kennedy, USNR. His courage, his calmness in the face of danger, his remarkable qualities of leadership were all tested in a way that few men are tested in their lifetime."

Maurice Kowal
Patrick McMahon
John Maguire
Barney Ross
Edmons Mauer

Lieutenant (j.g.) Kennedy, on a short visit home, is greeted by his friends Torby MacDonald and Chuck Spaulding in military fashion, in contrast to their strictly non-military bearing and appearance.

Charleston, South Carolina, where Kennedy was stationed prior to torpedo boat training in Meville, Rhode Island. He had hoped that Torby MacDonald, who was in attendance at the same training centre, could join him as executive officer under skipper Kennedy. But Kennedy was flown out to replace a commander already in action and the shafting he got, according to MacDonald, resulted in his nickname, "Shafty", by which he was known in the Solomon Islands.

"Native knows posit he can pilot 11 alive need small boat Kennedy."

Message carved into a coconut on Nauru and given to a Solomon Islander for delivery to US Forces. It was delivered to Lieutenant Wincote in New Georgia and next morning Kennedy had a reply:

"To Senior Officer, Nauru Is. Have just learned of your presence on Nauru Is. and also that two natives have taken news to Rendova. I strongly advise you return immediately to here in this canoe and by the time you arrive I will be in radio communication with authorities at Rendova and we can finalize plans to collect balance of your party. Will warn aviation of your crossing Ferguson Passage. Lt. Wincote."

On the night of August 1–2, 1943, Lieutenant (j.g.) Kennedy was leading three boats for a sweep on Japanese targets. Suddenly, at around 2.30 a.m., the look-out shouted, "Ship at two o'clock." But it was too late. A Japanese destroyer, coming out of the dark at high speed, bore down on the little ship and sliced it in half. The boat's fuel tanks, loaded with high-octane aviation fuel, exploded in a ball of fire and both the enemy and the US boats in formation were convinced that there were no survivors. Kennedy was slammed on his back, again injuring his spinal vertebrae that had prevented his earlier acceptance by the Navy. Gasoline was beginning to burn in the water and Kennedy saw that the front half of the boat was staying afloat. He also realized that some of his men had survived and, flashing a light in the darkness, he located ten of his twelve men and officers, all floating, in various degrees of shock and pain, wearing their life jackets.

One engineer was half burned, another near dead from swallowing gasoline, and gunner's mate Charles Harris, a Bostonian whose leg had been immobilized, was unable to swim. "For a man from Boston, you are really putting on some exhibition out here," Kennedy said, but he towed him to the floating hulk, where all of them clung to the wreckage.

The hulk was sinking and the next morning they decided to swim to an island three miles away, which they knew was free of Japanese. Pat MacMahon, the engineer whose legs were severely burned and who was only half-conscious, was unable to swim, so Kennedy, despite his own painfully crippled back, clenched the engineer's life belt strap between his teeth and towed him to the island. It took them five long hours.

Instantly Kennedy plunged back into the sea to search for help. All that night he swam, half in a daze, but found no passing US boats. In the morning he returned, in pain, hungry and exhausted. He collapsed. Six days later he and his crew were rescued.

"For extremely heroic conduct as commanding officer of Motor Torpedo Boat 109, following the collision and sinking of that vessel in the Pacific War Theater, August 1–2, 1943.

"Unmindful of personal danger, Lieutenant Kennedy unhesitatingly braved the difficulties and hazards of darkness to direct rescue operations, swimming many hours to secure aid and food after he had succeeded in getting his crew ashore.

"His courage, endurance and excellent leadership contributed to the saving of several lives and was in keeping with the highest traditions of the United States Naval Service."

Admiral Halsey's citation in awarding Lieutenant John F. Kennedy the Navy and Marine Corps Medal. He also received the Purple Heart. The carved coconut had a place of honour on his Oval Office desk once he achieved the presidency.

John F. Kennedy in the Solomon Islands.

Congressman

"When ships were sinking and young Americans were dying I firmly resolved to serve my country in peace, as honestly as I tried to serve in war."
JOHN F. KENNEDY, opening speech for 1946 campaign

Bunker Hill Day, June 17, 1946. The young John F. Kennedy, just back from the war, decided to run for the 11th District seat in the House of Representatives, a seat being vacated by James M. Curley, former Mayor of Boston and the nemesis of Kennedy's grandfather, Honey Fitz, who had also held the seat. Kennedy ran against eight other candidates. "He went into alleyways and climbed the stairs to tenement houses where politicians had never been seen before," says Dave Powers. This unprecedented campaign effort helped but it was his prestigious name which won him the seat. Young Jack was now a US Congressman, having assumed the mantle of his older brother. He was on his way to fulfil the promise of his name.

"We few, we happy few, we band of brothers
For he today that sheds his blood with me
Shall be my brother . . ."

Shakespeare's *Henry V* provided the young John Kennedy with an exhortation to his troops, few indeed, in the 1946 congressional campaign.

Congressional campaign. Dave Powers is centre right.

"We had never had an election like 1946 — if you did not have the word veteran beside your name you couldn't be elected dog-catcher. Now I took him over to speak to a group of Gold Star mothers — and this was a tough group to talk to — they had all lost a son in WW2. He did not have a prepared speech. It was just the two of us and several hundred women. He looked out and he said, 'I think I know how you ladies feel because my mother is a Gold Star mother too.' I've been in smoke-filled rooms with him from Maine to Alaska. But no reaction like this. He's surrounded by these Charlestown mothers and in the background I can hear them saying that he reminded them of their own son or a loved one they had lost."

DAVID F. POWERS

Senate Campaign 1952

Congressman Kennedy, soon to be the new Senator for the State of Massachusetts, surrounded by admirers during a "Tea".

In 1952 Congressman Kennedy decided to run for the Senate seat held by Henry Cabot Lodge since 1936. Senator Lodge, a scion of one of the families which had dominated Massachusetts since colonial days ("This is the good old Boston, the home of the bean and the cod, where the Lowells talk only to Cabots and the Cabots talk only to God") was not only considered unbeatable, but he was also, in that year, the national chairman of General Eisenhower's presidential campaign. Eisenhower won Massachusetts by a 208,000 majority, while Kennedy defeated Lodge by 70,737 votes.

"We were running teas and receptions in May, 5000 in Worcester, 4500 in Springfield. We had a tea and reception in the summertime at the Swampscott House on the North Shore. Ladies were invited from Swampscott, Revere, Lynn, Salem, Beverly — 7500 on a lovely Saturday afternoon in June. And you know we figured it out one day. Jack won by 70,737. I had a chart — we had thirty-three teas and receptions. We had some where there were 1000 — we had one in ward 9 in Boston for all black ladies, another one — a Greek affair — 750 or 1000 — but the thirty-three teas and receptions — added up to 70,000."
DAVID F. POWERS

"I think I can beat him."
JOHN F. KENNEDY

"It was those damn teas that killed me."
HENRY CABOT LODGE

There were the "Teas" and the television hit, "Coffee with the Kennedys", featuring the entire Kennedy cast, his mother Rose, his sisters and brothers. But the terrifying efficiency of the later political battles was already becoming apparent. Powers, gifted with an encyclopedic memory for names and faces, had prepared file cards on every leading citizen in every community known to vote Democratic. And two bright young men had joined the campaign: Kenny O'Donnell and Larry O'Brien, who would form some 350 Kennedy committees throughout the state and organize them into county and district groups. Bobby Kennedy, fresh out of the University of Virginia Law School, was named campaign manager and was able to cut his teeth for later, more far-reaching assignments. The teas were important, and so were the family's spirit and determination to win. But in the end it was the utter seriousness of the candidate in fighting this political battle that led to victory. Almost the only Democratic triumph in that election year, it astounded professional politicians throughout the country.

Husband

On September 12, 1953 United States Senator John F. Kennedy married Jacqueline Lee Bouvier, of Newport, Rhode Island. The wedding was the social event of the year, attracting huge crowds — 3000 people broke through police lines and nearly crushed the bride.

Inside St. Mary's Roman Catholic church in Newport, some 800 friends and notables had squeezed in to watch the Archbishop of Boston, Richard J. Cushing, perform the marriage ceremony and read out a special blessing from the Pope. More than 1200 guests attended the reception at "Jackie's" family home, Hammersmith Farm, and the crush was so great that it took nearly two hours for those in the reception line to greet the couple. Bobby Kennedy was his brother's best man and the Matron of Honour was Jackie's sister, Lee.

But the courtship had been difficult. The Congressman in 1952, the year they met, was spending every waking moment campaigning for the Senate in Massachusetts, and Jackie, who had been the Inquiring Photographer for the Washington *Times-Herald*, left for Europe shortly after the romance began. Said the future First Lady: "We didn't see each other for six months. . . . Then came six months when we were both back. . . . But it was still spasmodic because he spent half of each week in Massachusetts."

The couple's engagement party in June of 1953 included a scavenger hunt for the younger generation, which achieved some notoriety in staid Hyannis Port. The list included such items as a "monster from the sea", a "menu from a famous restaurant", the "longest object", and, most difficult of all a "show of courage". A salmon from the family freezer answered the first item, the menu was easy, but the next two were more difficult. Pat, a member of one of the teams together with Bobby and their cousin Joey, had noticed a parked bus in front of the station, and since the key was in the ignition she got in and drove it straight into the car park where the party was taking place. Joey's act of courage was even more risky. While looking for the menu, he noticed a policeman at lunch, with his hat next to him. He grabbed the hat, leapt into Bobby's car and off they went. That night, returning home from the party, they found three squad cars full of angry policemen waiting for them.

*"He'd call me from some oyster bar up there, with a great clinking of coins, to ask me
out to the movies the following Wednesday in Washington."*
JACQUELINE LEE BOUVIER

At the Democratic National Convention in 1956, Senator Kennedy, a surprise candidate, just loses the vice-presidential nomination. It was a stroke of luck, as President Eisenhower defeated Adlai Stevenson by a landslide, a fact which would have been blamed on Kennedy's Catholicism. The surprise near-victory strengthened Kennedy's resolve to run for the presidency.

"Mr. President, the time has come for the American people to be told the blunt truth about Indochina.

"I am reluctant to make any statement which may be misinterpreted as unappreciative of the gallant French struggle at Dien Bien Phu . . . or as partisan criticism of our Secretary of State . . . Nor do I wish to appear impetuous or an alarmist in my evaluation of the situation. But the speeches of President Eisenhower, Secretary Dulles, and others have left too much unsaid . . . and what has been left unsaid is the heart of the problem . . . For if the American people are, for the fourth time in this century, to travel the long and tortuous road of war — particularly a war which we now realize would threaten the survival of civilization — then I believe we have a right — a right which we should have hitherto exercised — to inquire in detail into the nature of the struggle in which we may become engaged, and the alternative to such struggle . . .

"Despite any wishful thinking to the contrary, it should be apparent that the popularity and prevalence of Ho Chi Minh and his following throughout Indochina would cause either partition or a coalition government to result in eventual domination by the Communists . . .

"I, for one, favor a policy of a 'united action' by many nations whenever necessary to achieve a military and political victory for the free world in that area, realizing full well that it may eventually require some commitment of our manpower.

"But to pour money, materiel, and men into the jungles of Indochina without at least a remote prospect of victory would be dangerously futile and self-destructive.

"If the French are unwilling to give up their interest there . . . then what is our interest there? In that event, we shall have no political or economic stake in preserving Indochina free from the Communists. Instead, we want to help maintain the independence of that area, free from Communist domination."

JOHN F. KENNEDY
The War in Indochina, Congressional Record, April 6, 1954

i

Robert Kennedy came to national attention as the Majority Counsel of the Select Committee on Improper Activities in the Labor or Management Field, better known as the "Labor Rackets Committee", which was chaired by Senator McClellan and on which Senator John F. Kennedy served. Robert had earlier been the Minority Counsel to Joe McCarthy's notorious Senate Subcommittee on Investigations, but he had finally renounced that witch-hunt with the outburst: "Until this moment, Senator, I think I never really gauged your cruelty or your recklessness. Have you no sense of decency, sir, at long last, have you left no sense of decency?" Now the Majority Counsel won wide praise, but his relentless pursuit of labour racketeers and dishonest executives earned him the "ruthless" image, which was to plague him throughout his political career.

MR. KENNEDY: Mr. Mattson, the employees that work for you, the drivers, do you pay them union scale?

MR. MATTSON: Union scale?

MR. KENNEDY: Union scale.

MR. MATTSON: This year I am not, no.

MR. KENNEDY: Do you pay them any lay-over?

MR. MATTSON: No.

MR. KENNEDY: Do you pay them any breakdown?

MR. MATTSON: No.

MR. KENNEDY: Do you pay them any meal allowance?

MR. MATTSON: No.

MR. KENNEDY: Do you pay them any lodging?

MR. MATTSON: No.

MR. KENNEDY: Do you pay them any holiday?

MR. MATTSON: No, only when they ask.

MR. KENNEDY: . . . Has the union complained about the fact that you pay no lay-over, you pay no union scale, you pay no breakdown, you pay no meal allowance, you pay no holiday when it is specified in the contract?

MR. MATTSON: No.

MR. KENNEDY: Whose back are you going to break?

MR. HOFFA: I don't remember it.

MR. KENNEDY: Well, whose back are you going to break Mr. Hoffa?

MR. HOFFA: It's a figure of speech. I don't know what you're talking about.

MR. KENNEDY: Has this been a profitable operation?

MR. HOFFA: You have the record. I think you could say that it was.

MR. KENNEDY: Approximately, how much do you think she made in that company since it was set up?

MR. HOFFA: I can't tell you, offhand, but a guess. I can give it to you this afternoon, if I can get it.

MR. KENNEDY: We have some figures here.

MR. HOFFA: Read them off, brother.

Robert Kennedy cross-examining witnesses before the Labor Rackets Committee

Senator

Ever since Harvard John F. Kennedy suffered from terrible back pains. When first running for the Senate, he had to be supported by crutches, a recurring need. Those who knew him well could tell when the sudden pain attacked him, yet his strength and courage was such that strangers never knew. The rocking chair, a therapeutic necessity, became a symbol of his presidency without ever detracting from his youthful and vigorous image.

"Just as I went into politics because Joe died, if anything happened to me tomorrow, my brother Bobby would run for my seat in the Senate. And if Bobby died Teddy would take over for him."

JOHN F. KENNEDY

"It is regrettable that the gap between the intellectual and the politician seems to be growing. Instead of synthesis, clash and discord now characterize the relations between the two groups much of the time. Authors, scholars, and intellectuals can praise every aspect of American society but the political. My desk is flooded with books, articles, and pamphlets criticizing Congress. But, rarely if ever, have I seen any intellectual bestow praise on either the political profession or any political body for its accomplishments, its ability, or its integrity — much less for its intelligence . . .

"But in fairness, the way of the intellectual is not altogether serene; in fact, so great has become popular suspicion that a recent survey of American intellectuals elicited from one of our foremost literary figures the guarded response, 'I ain't no intellectual.'

"It seems to me that the time has come for intellectuals and politicians alike to put aside those horrible weapons of modern internecine warfare, the barbed thrust, the acid pen, and, most sinister of all, the rhetorical blast. Let us not emphasize all on which we differ but all we have in common. Let us consider not what we fear separately but what we share together . . .

"The duty of the scholar, particularly in a republic such as ours, is to contribute his objective views and his sense of liberty to the affairs of his state and nation . . .

"Freedom of expression is not divisible into political expression and intellectual expression. The lock on the door of the legislature, the Parliament, or the assembly hall — by order of the King, the Commissar, or the Fuehrer — has historically been followed or preceded by a lock on the door of the university, the library, or the printshop. And if the first blow for freedom in any subjugated land is struck by a political leader, the second is struck by a book, a newspaper, or a pamphlet . . .

" 'Don't teach my boy poetry,' an English mother recently wrote the Provost of Harrow. 'Don't teach my boy poetry; he is going to stand for Parliament.' Well, perhaps she was right — but if more politicians knew poetry, and more poets knew politics, I am convinced the world would be a little better place in which to live on this commencement day of 1955."

JOHN F. KENNEDY
Harvard University Commencement Address 1955

Senator Kennedy on Capitol Hill and in his Senate office.

The Senator leaving his home on N Street in Georgetown, Washington DC, in 1958.

The marriage was to be marred by pain and tragedy. In October 1954 Senator Kennedy underwent a lumbar spine operation, which was a failure. An infection set in and, while his wife and family prayed for him, he received the last rites. He survived, but in February of 1955 he submitted himself, in spite of all the inherent risk, to a second operation. This time the surgeons succeeded. His period of recuperation was lengthy and painful, but he used the time to write his second book, *Profiles in Courage,* with the help of Jackie and his legislative assistant Theodore "Ted" Sorensen, a work which won him the Pulitzer Prize.

On August 23, 1956 their first child, a girl, was still-born, but in November of 1957 Jackie gave birth to a healthy girl, Caroline. Life was beginning to look promising again.

The Christmas card, 1959.

Dear Jacques

The picture we would like for our Xmas card is on the top page below — with a line of X's. I have marked across the top —

It is on page 129A 5 — # 11 H —

If possible could you replace the baby's face with the one directly above t, marked with 2 X's — 129A 5 #12 — as she is slightly better in the above picture

— thanks — Jackie K

The Georgetown house.

"I have filled the Georgetown house with eighteenth-century furniture, which I love, and my pictures — the drawings I collect . . . but I haven't made it completely all my own because I never want a house where you have to say to your children 'Don't touch' or where your husband isn't comfortable . . . there are lots of little things . . . there are also big comfortable chairs and the tables that every politician needs next to his chair, where he can put papers, coffee cups, ash trays."

JACQUELINE KENNEDY

The nursery.

Having a wonderful time
in the sea, off the family
compound in Hyannis
Port, 1958.

THE SEARCH FOR VOTES AND HANDS TO SHAKE

Early Campaign and the Primaries

Senator Kennedy on an early campaign trip in Wisconsin. There were few in those days who listened.

"I am announcing today my candidacy for the presidency of the United States . . . For eighteen years I have been in the service of the United States, first as a naval officer in the Pacific during World War II and for the past fourteen years as a member of Congress. In the last twenty years I have traveled in nearly every continent and country — from Leningrad to Saigon, from Bucharest to Lima. From all this I have developed an image of America as fulfilling a noble and historic role as the defender of freedom in a time of maximum peril — and of the American people as confident, courageous and persevering. It is with this image that I begin this campaign."

JOHN F. KENNEDY, January 2, 1960

"In a recent survey American mothers were asked what their ambitions were for their sons. Seventy per cent replied that they hoped he would become President of the United States, but only ten per cent wanted them to be politicians. Which reminds me of the great Artemus, who said that he was not a politician and his other habits were good also."
JOHN F. KENNEDY

"In some towns, it was difficult to find anybody who was willing to shake hands, and most of the people who did talk to Kennedy were schoolchildren too young to vote."
KENNETH O'DONNELL

". . . Any man who goes into a primary isn't fit to be president. You have to be crazy to go into a primary. A primary, now, is worse than the torture on the rack. It's all right to enter a primary by accident, or because you don't know any better, but by forethought . . .?"
HUBERT H. HUMPHREY

A crowd of schoolchildren attracted the candidate. A minute after this photograph was taken he jumped on a tractor parked by the roadside and made a short speech about democracy and voting. They might tell their fathers and mothers.

"Mr. President, May 17, 1960 marked the end of an era — an era of illusion, the illusion that personal good will is a substitute for hard, carefully prepared bargaining on concrete issues, the illusion that good intentions and pious principles are a substitute for strong creative leadership.

"For on May 17, 1960 the long-awaited, highly publicized summit conference collapsed. That collapse was the direct result of Soviet determination to destroy the talks. The insults and distortions of Mr. Khrushchev and the violence of his attacks shocked all Americans, and united the country in admiration for the dignity and self-control of President Eisenhower. Regardless of party, all of us deeply resented Russian abuse of this nation and its President, and all of us shared a common disappointment at the failure of the conference. Nevertheless, it is imperative that we, as a nation, rise above our resentment and frustration to a critical re-examination of the events at Paris and their meaning for America . . .

"The harsh facts of the matter are that the effort to eliminate world tensions and end the cold war through a summit meeting . . . was doomed to failure long before the U-2 ever fell on Soviet soil. This effort was doomed to failure because we have failed for the past eight years to build the positions of long-term strength essential to successful negotiation. It was doomed because we were unprepared with new policies or new programs for the settlement of outstanding substantive issues . . .

"Trunkloads of papers, I am told, were sent to Paris, but no new plans or positions were included . . . Our allies and our own people had been misled into believing that there was some point to holding a summit conference . . .

"But the truth of the matter is that we were not prepared . . .

"If the 1960 campaign should degenerate into a contest of who can talk toughest to Khrushchev, or which party is the 'party of war' or the 'party of appeasement', or which candidate can tell the American voters what they want to hear, rather than what they need to hear, or who is soft on Communism, or who can be hardest on foreign aid, then, in my opinion, it makes very little difference who the winners are in July and in November; the American people and the whole free world will be the losers."

JOHN F. KENNEDY
A Time of Decision, Congressional Record, June 14, 1960

Early in 1960 Senator Kennedy, his wife, and personal aide Dave Powers, arrived in Oregon at dusk for a campaign appearance. The Senator was not yet the frontrunner, simply one of five candidates for the Democratic presidential nomination. Four people came to welcome him, as opposed to the tumultuous scenes that were to occur only months later.

In 1961, in the Oval Office, I asked the President to autograph my earlier book. ''Let me show you my favorite picture,'' he said, stabbing at the photograph above. ''No one remembers today.''

Whose woods are these I think I know
His house is in the village though;
He will not see me stopping here
To watch his woods fill up with snow.

My little horse must think it queer
To stop without a farmhouse near,
Between the woods and frozen lake
The darkest evening of the year.

He gives his harness bells a shake
To ask if there is some mistake.
The only other sound's the sweep
Of easy wind and downy flake.

The woods are lovely, dark, and deep.
But I have promises to keep,
And miles to go before I sleep,
And miles to go before I sleep.

ROBERT FROST, "Stopping by Woods on a Snowy Evening"

Jacqueline, Senator Kennedy and Steve Smith at breakfast in a local diner in Oregon. That was the campaign team.

*"We might fly to Oregon for three or four days. Then we would get up at 6.30 a.m.
and go to breakfasts, luncheons, dinners in different places. Once in Wisconsin we
drove fifty miles in below-zero weather and had to leave our car at two or three stops
along the way."*

JACQUELINE KENNEDY

A reflective moment in Coos Bay, Oregon. This is my favourite photograph of John F. Kennedy.

The Primaries

Parkersburg, West Virginia.

Charleston, West Virginia.

Jackie autographing programmes, Wisconsin.

Charleston, West Virginia.

Senator Kennedy in Charleston, West Virginia, towards the end of the primary.

The religious issue, Kennedy's Catholicism, had started to raise its ugly head in the Wisconsin primary. Simple prejudice and real ignorance of the religion, especially among country people, was only one part of that problem, the more worrisome aspect being the "Al Smith" syndrome, the bugaboo that a Catholic could not be elected. Al Smith, a colourful New York Democrat and a Catholic, had been defeated by a landslide in 1928, a fact which was squarely blamed on his religion.

One Wisconsin paper, discussing the primary fight, had the word Catholic twenty times in a fifteen-paragraph article, and the *Milwaukee Journal,* the state's most influential newspaper, divided election-night figures into three columns, Democrat, Republican and Catholic. But while it was a serious issue in Wisconsin, religion became the *only* issue, the burning issue, in the next state primary, West Virginia.

The few who came to see the candidate simply stared at him suspiciously, unwilling to shake his hand, unwilling to ask *the* question . . . until the candidate addressed the problem himself. "When it first happened," says Dave Powers, "the crowd was stunned and so was I." "Nobody asked me if I was a Catholic when I joined the United States Navy . . . and nobody asked my brother if he was a Catholic or a Protestant before he climbed into an American bomber plane to fly his last mission." "Pretty good talker," said one of the crowd. "Good-looking feller, isn't he?" said his friend.

"You shake hundreds of hands in the afternoon and hundreds more at night. You get so tired you catch yourself laughing and crying at the same time. But you pace yourself and you get through it. You just look at it as something you have to do. You knew it would come and you knew it was worth it."

JACQUELINE KENNEDY

The well-tested teas and coffees for ladies were being introduced again by the Kennedy women.

"There's only one problem. He's a Catholic. That's our God-damned problem!"
Campaign worker for Kennedy in West Virginia

Senator Kennedy at Mills College, California, campaigning between primaries.

Jacqueline Kennedy and a longshoreman during a union hall campaign stop in Oregon.

"Will my real opponent for the presidential nomination in West Virginia please stand up?"
JOHN F. KENNEDY

Jacqueline Kennedy quilting. *Right:* Reporter Bob Healy of the *Boston Globe* and Pierre Salinger with the candidate.

John F. Kennedy eating his customary lunch, Boston clam chowder, while giving an interview. *Right:* Staff conference on board.

Jackie reading Jack Kerouac's *The Dharma Bums*.

The by now famous Kennedy plane, the *Caroline*, a converted Corvair, was the one oasis of calm in an otherwise hectic schedule. It served as a place of rest, an office, a restaurant and as the campaign headquarters in the air. Occasionally reporters would come along. The log of the *Caroline* in a five-week period between May 20 and June 27 shows Kennedy flying from Oregon to Libertyville Illinois (to see Adlai Stevenson), to Hyannis Port, to Washington DC, to New Jersey, New York, Washington State (the opposite end of the country), to New Mexico, San Francisco, Chicago, Michigan (to see G. Mennen Williams), Colorado, Minnesota, Colorado again, New Jersey again, Boston, New York again, New Jersey again, Pennsylvania, Washington DC, Massachusetts and finally to Montana for the state convention.

John F. Kennedy getting dressed shortly before arriving in California.

Of the seven primaries Senator Kennedy entered, New Hampshire, Indiana, Maryland, Nebraska, Wisconsin, West Virginia and Oregon, he won them all, and decisively. Still, when he won six out of ten counties in Wisconsin, a state in which Hubert Humphrey was known as the "third Senator", the press, instead of crediting Kennedy with an overwhelming victory, called it a failure, so exaggerated had become their idea of success. Senator Humphrey, again the opponent in West Virginia, had become the clear frontrunner in that state, purely because of the religious issue. The early polls, which had given Kennedy and Humphrey a 70%–30% success rating, had reversed themselves in these exact figures, after the Catholic issue had become a matter of public debate in Wisconsin. Senator Humphrey, moreover, was no longer the real opponent, his fate having been sealed in Wisconsin, but he had become the stalking horse, the "stop Kennedy" front man, for Lyndon Johnson, Stuart Symington and Adlai Stevenson, none of whom entered the contest, a fact Kennedy drove strongly home to the voters.

Senator Humphrey's campaign was inept, at best. A respected member of the liberal establishment, his policies differed little from those of Senator Kennedy. He could not and would not stir up the religious issue. Still, the music of "Give Us That Old Time Religion", a well-known ditty, was used in his campaign song. Short of money himself, he used the Kennedy money as an issue, accusing his opponent of buying votes, a matter which stirred up little concern in a state where vote buying, especially in sheriff's races, was not unusual. His major television address, a telethon the night before election day, was an unmitigated disaster. Using an open telephone line, rather than pre-screened questions, one of his first callers was a shrill-voiced woman, who screamed "You git out of West Virginia, Mr. Humphrey. You git out, do you hear?" The balance of the programme was not much of an improvement.

Kennedy's head-on confrontation of the religious issue and his tireless campaign among the poor (he had come to the Humphrey–Kennedy debate carrying a government food ration package to demonstrate its shortcomings), were effective. He also recruited Franklin Roosevelt Jr., son of the President who was a saintly figure in the state, and a Protestant, and he campaigned tirelessly on Kennedy's behalf, finally clinching the issue. The final tally was 212,000 for Kennedy against 136,000 for Humphrey, a 60%–40% ratio. It was a momentous victory. In a state with a five per cent Catholic population, it laid to rest the argument as to whether a Catholic could win the presidency, at least until after the forthcoming Democratic National Convention. It was this victory that clinched the first ballot nomination for Senator Kennedy there.

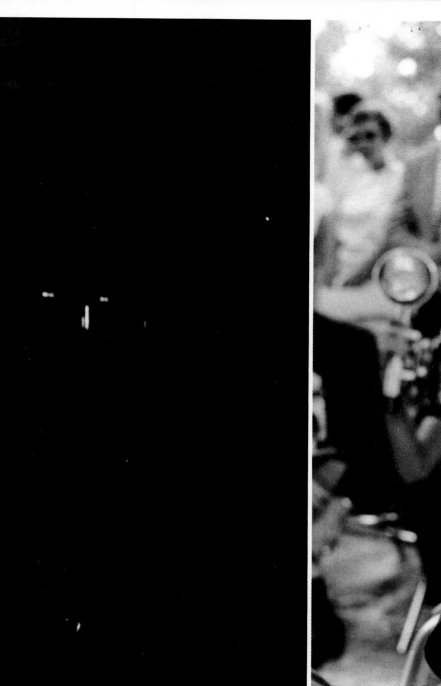

Senator Kennedy in Nebraska.

"Caroline's first words were plane, good-
bye and New Hampshire, and she recently
learned to say Wisconsin and West
Virginia. Any day now she is expected to
come out with Maryland and Oregon."
JOHN F. KENNEDY

A TIME FOR GREATNESS
THE JOHN F. KENNEDY STORY

KENNEDY
FOR
PRESIDENT
Oregon Primary May 20, 1960

TRIUMPH IN LOS ANGELES

The Democratic Convention

Senator Kennedy addressing the combined Massachusetts–Texas caucus, a critical challenge which he carried off with humour and ease.

"Senator Smathers has been one of my most valuable counselors at crucial moments — in '52 when I was thinking of running for the US Senate, I went to Senator Smathers and said George, what do you think? Don't do it . . . it's a bad year. So I defeated Henry Cabot Lodge by 70,737 in '56. I said George, do you think I should run for vice president? Smathers replied — you have a good chance — I ran and lost. In '60, I was wondering about entering the West Virginia primary. Smathers said that state you can't possibly carry and actually the only time I really got nervous in Los Angeles was just before the balloting when George said it looks pretty good for you."

JOHN F. KENNEDY

A difficult moment at the Montana caucus.

A political convention, Democrat or Republican, is more akin to a carnival than to a serious political rally. The 1960 convention was no exception. It was my first. 4509 delegates were expected, 4750 reporters were accredited and the army of party officials, staff workers, groupies and the just plain curious was inestimable. The Biltmore hotel in downtown Los Angeles was the nerve centre of the convention. The lobby, where legendary political figures were rubbing shoulders with the gawkers, also featured two rival Puerto Rican delegations in loud, Latin costumes vying for attention with steel drums and guitars.

Girls dressed in candy-striped outfits and wearing boaters were handing out badges and literature for the various contenders, as well as Pepsi (Symington), PT 109 tie clasps (Kennedy) and the collected speeches of Adlai Stevenson. A man brandishing a ''Massachusetts for Johnson'' placard turned out to be from Lubbock, Texas, and an enormous fat man was waving a ''Texas is big for Kennedy'' sign. There were men in cowboy suits and others sporting Eskimo costumes, neither looking authentic. Outside the lunacy proliferated in a sea of waving banners. ''Stop Khrushchev'', ''Fear God'', ''Vote for Prohibition'' competed with ''Back Jack'', and a local nightclub owner driving by with eight nearly naked girls almost stampeded the crowd. But the work of the convention *was* serious.

Robert Kennedy at work with delegates.

Upstairs in suite 8315, Robert Kennedy's headquarters, the activity was feverish, but subdued. The staff had returned from the spring primary wars as veteran political strategists, and under the direction of Bobby Kennedy, that experience was now put to work. Kennedy had come to the convention with 600 votes pledged to him and he needed a further 161 to get the nomination. He began a tireless round of state caucuses, visiting every delegation that would have him, and meeting the party leaders individually, while Teddy, Steve Smith, Kenny O'Donnell and Larry O'Brien as well as the older Kennedy loyalists such as John Bailey, the shrewd

Connecticut state chairman, and Governor Ribicoff of the same state, some forty men in all, were each assigned a state delegation to work with. They were given file cards, which listed the names, professions, marital status, religion and whatever other information was useful to help them in their task of cajoling reluctant delegates into voting for Kennedy. Every hour the delegate score was tabulated and adjusted, and, when it came to final balloting that score turned out to be incredibly accurate. No one slept much, relaxation was forbidden and no one was ever out of touch with suite 8315 from Friday through to the final ballot. But there were hurdles still to be overcome.

Senator Kennedy visiting state caucuses.

Stuart Symington demonstration. *Below:* Kenny O'Donnell taking instructions from Senator Kennedy. *Below right:* Steve Smith.

Startled Kennedy supporters on the floor.

Senator Kennedy never set foot in the convention hall until the night of his nomination. He operated out of suite 9333, attending state caucuses and receiving political leaders, but at night and for diverse reasons, such as avoiding the demands of thousands of reporters, he would slip out to his secret hideaway, a penthouse at 522 North Rossmore Avenue, owned by Jack Haley. Only ten minutes from the Biltmore and the convention hall, the place was ideal, especially as a secluded drive had direct access to the elevators. Four telephone lines had been installed, one to Evelyn Lincoln, his secretary, one to suite 8315 and two open lines. All this worked well, until the day of the nomination. Returning early and looking forward to some relaxation prior to the long night ahead, Kennedy found the street blocked by television trucks, cables, reporters and curious onlookers. The newshounds had spotted him. So he entered the house from the front . . . and left through the back.

"One of the back bedrooms had a fire escape. He (Kennedy) could just go down the fire escape and then there was a wall. Oh, I'd say the wall was about five and a half, six feet. We told the chauffeur to get the car and drive around the back of the block and stay there . . . (Kennedy) went out and went down the fire escape. Then he took that wall, and I held my breath because of his back. He leaped over it and ran through the bushes and everything else and got into the car."
DAVID F. POWERS

Stevenson demonstration.

Henry Fonda directing the Stevenson demonstration.

"Do not reject this man who has made us all proud to be Democrats. Do not leave this prophet without honor in his own party . . . This favorite son of mine, I submit to you Adlai Stevenson of Illinois."

EUGENE McCARTHY
nominating Stevenson

The early hours of a political convention are an endless succession of tedious speeches and good-natured rival demonstrations. The 1960 convention differed in that, ever since the delegates had assembled at the Sports Arena, an ominous crowd had gathered outside the hall shouting: "We want Stevenson. We want Stevenson." The crowd included pinstriped businessmen, jean-clad youth, and babycarriage-pushing mothers. The demonstration had started quietly, but by the evening thousands of banner-waving men and women had become unruly and shrill, frenzied and angry. Stevenson himself, twice the defeated presidential candidate of the Democratic Party, professed not to be a candidate and seemed to mean it. He was the revered leader of the party's liberal wing and his followers would not accept a "no". Always ambivalent, he had gone to the convention the next day and taken his seat as an Illinois delegate, the only major leader to do so. He had been greeted with overwhelming applause and affection. Now his "no" turned to "maybe" and then, under pressure from his supporters, to an active search for delegates at this late hour. It was a short-lived attempt, for his own state of Illinois turned him down, and although he knew there was no chance, he never stopped his supporters, and he never stopped the rumours which are the lifeblood of any convention. It was a tense time. On the third day, the Wednesday, before the nomination, the Stevenson demonstrators were slipping into the hall, slowly filling the galleries, a nearly impossible feat in an arena in which every seat was numbered and jealously guarded. I was standing in the hall listening to Eugene McCarthy's magnificent speech nominating Stevenson, when suddenly a roar broke out from the balconies and thousands of demonstrators poured on to the floor as well as into the galleries, screaming, squirming, hysterically snake dancing, chanting "We want Stevenson, we want Stevenson." Tearing loose state banners, pushing aside protestors objecting to the unruliness, they were no longer demonstrators but became an unruly mob. McCarthy tried to calm them, the lights were turned off, but nothing could stop them and the demonstration, according to my notes, lasted twenty-three minutes. It seemed a lifetime and as a former Stevenson Democrat, I found it a sad finale to the political career of a gentle, thoughtful and fiercely admired man.

A concerned Senator Kennedy.

Eunice Shriver, Joan and Ethel Kennedy during Kennedy for President demonstration.

In spite of the Stevenson, and other, noisy demonstrations, John F. Kennedy won on the first ballot. The official results were: Senator John F. Kennedy of Massachusetts 806, Senator Lyndon B. Johnson of Texas 409, Senator Stuart Symington of Missouri 86, Adlai Stevenson of Illinois 79½, Governor Robert Meyner of New Jersey 43, Senator Hubert Humphrey of Minnesota 41½, Senator George Smathers of Florida 30, Governor Ross Barnett of Mississippi 23, Governor Herschel Loveless of Iowa 1½ and Governors Pat Brown of California, Orval Faubus of Arkansas and Albert Rosselini of Washington ½ vote each.

That night the victorious candidate addressed the convention in a short and not very remarkable speech. But people were weeping, a man waved a 1932 newspaper describing Franklin Roosevelt's nomination, the state standards were thrust forward. The Democrats had a candidate for president. Also that night there was a quiet celebration at the Kennedy command bungalow, only yards from the convention hall. It was a hushed affair. Staff and family were there, the leaders of Democratic politics had come to pay homage, but there was no champagne, no joviality. It was almost a sacred recognition of the new leader. For the first time I realized the significance of the truly momentous and historic occasion I had been lucky enough to participate in, a significance which in eighteen-hour days had never truly implanted itself on my mind.

Prendergast, Harriman and DeSapio of
New York State (top), and other state
delegates during Kennedy balloting.

Pat Kennedy Lawford, a California
delegate, cheering the result.

A DAY TO REMEMBER

Choosing a Vice President

The Democratic presidential nominee in his suite, No. 9333.

What the Democratic nominee wanted to talk to Lyndon Johnson about was the offer of the vice presidency. Only days before, when the exchange between the two men had been bitter and personal, Kennedy had said at the Texas–Massachusetts caucus, ''So I come here today full of admiration for Senator Johnson, full of affection for him, strongly in support of him for majority leader, and I'm confident that in that position we're going to be able to work together.'' He had said it with a smile, but the smile had been forced. Now apparently he had changed his mind.

I had come early that fateful morning, Thursday July 14, which was to decide the future of America for eight years to come, to Senator Kennedy's suite 9333 and was surprised by the large group that was already assembled. The suite was a series of seven rooms, one following the other in railroad fashion, but all doors to the corridor were locked and there was only one entrance. Here in the first room were political leaders representing the diverse factions of the Democratic Party, some privileged columnists and staff, milling about, waiting to see the Democratic nominee. I walked through to the bedroom, the last in the row of rooms, where Senator Kennedy was already on the telephone. One by one, each group of leaders, especially the long list of vice-presidential hopefuls, entered, was given word of the decision against them and left. Stuart Symington was the first of those and Orville Freeman the last.

The 8 a.m. call to Lyndon Johnson. Jim McShane (right) and Chuck Roche, an aide (left).

8 a.m. "When I called Lyndon, his wife Ladybird answered. She said that he was asleep, but she'd wake him. I told Lyndon that I wanted to talk to him, and we agreed to meet in his room in two hours."
JOHN F. KENNEDY

10.45 a.m. "One of the first party leaders I saw was Governor David Lawrence of Pennsylvania, whose delegation had supported my nomination. A week before the convention I called him and asked, 'Governor, what are you going to do?' He replied, 'Jack, you won't be sorry about what I'm going to do.' I gave Governor Lawrence my suggestion for the vice presidency. He said that if this was my decision, he would back it."

JOHN F. KENNEDY

11.30 a.m. "Governors Abe Ribicoff and Mike DiSalle of Ohio also supported Lyndon Johnson for the vice presidency. Both have been devoted friends. Abe Ribicoff was the first man who thought I could be president. After the 1956 convention, when I lost the vice-presidential nomination by 20½ votes, he said to me, 'Jack, four years from now, we'll go all the way.'"

JOHN F. KENNEDY

Left, from top to bottom: Senators Symington and Smathers leaving the Kennedy suite.
Kennedy with Governor David Lawrence (pointing finger).
With Governors Abe Ribicoff and (background) Mike DiSalle.
Governor Soapy Williams of Michigan with bow-tie talking to Terry Sanford of North Carolina; Kennedy with Chester Bowles.

10.15 a.m. *"I asked Lyndon if he were available for the vice presidency. He told me that he was. He then suggested that I discuss the matter with various party leaders while he conferred with his own advisers."*

JOHN F. KENNEDY

3.15 p.m. *"Governor Orville Freeman of Minnesota had been in a tough spot. Senator Hubert Humphrey was for Stevenson. Minnesota's junior Senator, Eugene McCarthy, first came out for Johnson and then nominated Stevenson. But Governor Freeman stuck with me through all the rough hours. When I told him that Lyndon was my choice, he may have been disappointed. But he accepted it with grace and said he would continue with me all the way."*

JOHN F. KENNEDY

Kennedy with Governor Orville Freeman (second from right) and others.

4.30 p.m. "After discussion with some of the party's leaders, it was agreed that Lyndon would be the strongest possible candidate for vice president. I called him on the phone again, and he said, 'Jack, if you want me to run, I'll do it.' After I had talked to Lyndon, I heard that certain other party leaders, including some in labor, were unhappy. I sent my brother Bobby down to Lyndon to tell him there might be a fight on the convention floor. He told Bobby, 'If Jack wants me for vice president, I'm willing to make a fight for it.' I told Bobby that if Lyndon was ready to fight, so was I. I informed Clark Clifford, Senator Stuart Symington's adviser, of my decision. I also told Senator Henry Jackson of Washington, who had been under serious consideration. Then we made the announcement."

JOHN F. KENNEDY

When word got out that Johnson had been chosen to run for the vice presidency, it caused an uproar in both the liberal and conservative wings of the party. The liberals such as G. Mennen "Soapy" Williams and Chester Bowles, who had supported Kennedy from the beginning, and various labour leaders, were furious at the betrayal of principle. Johnson's conservative friends were equally adamant, with Sam Rayburn, the Speaker of the House and a fellow Texan, almost ordering Johnson to reject the offer if it came. Bobby, who could take much credit for the victory, who had worked so hard and knew the mood of the Democrats perhaps better than anyone, was also strongly opposed to Johnson, and the emotional O'Donnell in a later memoir wrote that he "could have belted" David Lawrence, the influential Pennsylvania leader, when that wily politician said to Kennedy: "Johnson has the strength where you need it most."

The vice presidency is not considered a great political prize in America. John Nance Garner, a colourful vice president under Franklin Roosevelt, had said it "wasn't worth a pitcher of warm spit". Hubert Humphrey would say ruefully: "There is a story about the mother who had two sons. One went to sea and the other became vice president, and neither was ever heard of again." British Prime Minister Harold Macmillan told Kennedy that Eisenhower never let "Nixon on the place", meaning that he was excluded from the private functions of the White House. Moreover, Kennedy was forty-three and in the prime of health now, and Johnson, by accepting the vice presidency, was giving up the more powerful post of Majority Leader of the Senate. But somehow the one-heartbeat-away-from-the-presidency position seems irresistible. Later, even Robert Kennedy would seek it under Johnson, a man whom by that time he detested. So I was much surprised when I heard Kennedy ask Johnson if he would serve, and even more surprised when Johnson said he would.

Senator Johnson, Robert F. Kennedy and John F. Kennedy prior to the official announcement.

6.30 p.m. "This had been a day to remember. It also had been a long and difficult one, which involved a number of decisions, many of them contested. But throughout this day — as through all the others before it — my brother had been constantly at my side, giving me his support and counsel. One campaign had ended. Another was now about to begin."

JOHN F. KENNEDY

"One would just look the other in the eye, and there was the message. They had a great habit with the thumb, just a signal with the thumb. The Senator would look at Bob and thumb, and the message would be in."

JAMES McSHANE, investigator for Robert Kennedy's Labor Rackets Committee and personal bodyguard for
Senator Kennedy during the convention

". . . I think the American people expect more from us than cries of indignation and attack. The times are too grave, the challenge too urgent, the stakes too high to permit the customary passions of political debate. We are not here to curse the darkness, but to light the candle that can guide us . . . Today our concern must be with the future. For the world is changing. The old era is ending. The old ways will not do . . . The problems are not all solved and the battles are not all won — and we stand today on the edge of a New Frontier — the frontier of the 1960s — a frontier of unknown opportunities and perils — a frontier of unfulfilled hopes and threats . . .

"The New Frontier of which I speak is not a set of promises — it is a set of challenges. It sums up, not what I intend to offer the American people, but what I intend to ask of them. It appeals to their pride, not their pocketbook — it holds out the promise of more sacrifice instead of more security . . .

"Can a nation organized and governed such as ours endure? That is the real question. Have we the nerve and the will? Can we carry through in an age where we will witness not only new breakthroughs in weapons of destruction — but also a race for mastery of the sky and the rain, the ocean and the tides, the far side of space and the inside of men's minds . . .

"It has been a long road . . . to this crowded convention city. Now begins another long journey . . .

"Give me your hand, your voice and your vote."

JOHN F. KENNEDY
Acceptance Speech, July 15, 1960

Senator Kennedy on the flight from Los Angeles to Boston with Robert's son, Bobby.

Ethel Kennedy reading to her children.

On Friday, July 15, the convention switched to the Coliseum, a 100,000-capacity baseball stadium, where the Dodgers normally caucused. It was the Democrats' equivalent of a love feast. John F. Kennedy was surrounded by his family and all the leaders of the factions which had tried so hard to defeat him had their turn at speaking. Humphrey, Symington, Johnson, Stevenson and Eleanor Roosevelt, vice-presidential hopeful Henry Jackson, now the party's own chairman, and numerous others all took their turn, proclaiming Democratic unity and praising the standard bearer. Joseph P. Kennedy watched the show from the home of Henry R. Luce, the powerful publisher, and Richard Nixon, the Republican candidate, watched his rival from Washington DC. Jacqueline Kennedy was at home in Hyannis Port, pregnant with John-John. When the nominee's turn came late in the night he announced the "New Frontier", a phrase which was to characterize the administration.

The return from Los Angeles to Boston on July 17 on American Airlines' Kennedy Special was a joyous occasion. After two long years of daily, grinding campaigning, behind-the-scenes juggling, euphoric moments and deep disappointments, the Democratic standard bearer could look forward to some rest, some time with his family and his beloved Caroline, for in August the campaigning would be subdued, to pick up again at a furious pace in September. The four-hour-and-fifty-eight-minute journey across the country was symbolic of the times ahead. A crowd of 15,000 people greeted us on arrival, the largest we had had to date. But there was still work to be done. I remember one morning during that August when the sitting room of the Senator's house had been given over to a minorities leadership meeting, with Poles, Hungarians and Slovaks all telephoning in different languages. An astonished Jacqueline Kennedy, coming down for breakfast, tried the porch, where a dozen Boston supporters and their wives were waiting enveloped in cigar smoke to pay their respects to the presidential candidate. Shaking hands all around, the future First Lady then tried the dining room, where the candidate, deep in a round of delicate negotiations, waved her frantically away. The kitchen, now the only room left, was occupied by Salinger, briefing thirty reporters. It wasn't privacy or total relaxation. Still, there were moments of peace and reflection, the last for some months, perhaps years to come.

"With a deep sense of duty and high resolve, I accept your nomination."
JOHN F. KENNEDY

Triumphant arrival in Boston.

THE LONG ROAD TO VICTORY

The Presidential Campaign

"I think that we should concern ourselves in the coming months and years not only with our relations abroad, not only with the face that we present to the world, but also with the kind of society that we are developing here. What we are speaks louder than what we say, as Emerson said."

JOHN F. KENNEDY

JOHN F. KENNEDY SCHEDULE
MISSOURI–KANSAS OCTOBER 22, 1960 (Saturday)

3.00 a.m.	Arrive Lambert Airport St. Louis. Motorcade to Park Plaza Motel.
9.15 a.m.	Democratic Breakfast, Park Plaza Motel.
9.30 a.m.	Depart Park Plaza Motel by motorcade.
9.35 a.m.	Arrive Crestwood Shopping Center & Rally.
10.05 a.m.	Depart Crestwood Shopping Center.
10.50 a.m.	Arrive Northland Shopping Center. Rally.
11.20 a.m.	Depart Northland Shopping Center.
11.30 a.m.	Arrive Lambert Airport.
12.00 noon	Depart Lambert Airport for Joplin, Mo.
12.20 p.m.	Arrive Joplin. Airport Rally.
1.05 p.m.	Depart Joplin for Wichita, Kansas.
2.15 p.m.	Arrive Wichita Airport. Motorcade to Lawrence Stadium.
2.30 p.m.	Arrive Lawrence Stadium.
3.00 p.m.	Depart Lawrence Stadium for Wichita Airport.
3.30 p.m.	Leave Wichita Airport.
4.30 p.m.	Arrive Richards-Gebaur Air Force Base, Grandview. Motorcade to Truman Shopping Center.
4.45 p.m.	Arrive Truman Shopping Center, Grandview. Rally.
5.15 p.m.	Depart Truman Shopping Center.
5.45 p.m.	Arrive Muehlebach Hotel. Rest and Dinner alone.
8.00 p.m.	Depart hotel for Auditorium.
8.30 p.m.	Television Speech from Auditorium.
9.15 p.m.	Depart Auditorium by motorcade for Kansas City, Kansas.
9.30 p.m.	Arrive Fund Raising Dinner at Shawnee Mission East High School, Kansas City, Kansas.
9.45 p.m.	Depart Fund Raising Dinner for Richards-Gebaur Air Force Base.
10.00 p.m.	Arrive Richards-Gebaur Air Force Base.
10.15 p.m.	Depart for Green Bay, Wisconsin.
12.45 a.m.	Arrive Green Bay.

This schedule is typical of those for the days before and after October 22. It proved impossible to achieve the precision demanded by these schedules, and by the end of the day we would be late, sometimes an hour, sometimes two. Sleep and hot meals were not considered necessary during the campaign.

A TIME FOR GREATNESS

KENNEDY
FOR
PRESIDENT

viii

"So it is apparently necessary for me to state once again — not what kind of church I believe in, for that should be important only to me — but what kind of America I believe in . . .

"I believe in an America where the separation of church and state is absolute —

"I believe in an America that is officially neither Catholic, Protestant nor Jewish . . . and where religious liberty is so indivisible that an act against one church is treated as an act against all.

"Finally, I believe in an America where religious intolerance will someday end — where all men and all churches are treated as equal . . . where there is no Catholic vote, no anti-Catholic vote . . . where Catholics, Protestants and Jews will refrain from those attitudes of disdain and division which have so often marred . . . the American ideal of brotherhood. That is the kind

of America in which I believe . . .

"I am not the Catholic candidate for president. I am the Democratic Party's candidate for president who happens also to be a Catholic . . .

"If the time should ever come when my office would require me to either violate my conscience or violate the national interest, then I would resign the office . . . but I do not intend to apologize for these views nor do I intend to disavow either my views or my church in order to win this election.

"If I should lose on the real issues, I shall return to my seat in the Senate, satisfied that I had tried my best and was fairly judged. But if this election is decided on the basis that 40 million Americans lost their chance of being president on the day they were baptized, then it is the whole nation that will be the loser."

JOHN F. KENNEDY
Speech to the Ministerial Association, Houston, Texas, September 12, 1960

The Television Debates

How do I love thee
   Let me count the ways
I love thee as a tourist
   In Manhattan seeing plays
! love thee as a father
   In Virginia with your child
I love thee as a fullback
   In New England running wild
I love thee as a golfer
   When you're playing in Palm Beach
I love thee as a scholar
   Overseas to make a speech
I love thee as a brother
   With your sisters on a trip
I love thee as a comic
   When you pull a clever quip
I love thee as a sailor
   In Hyannis on your boat
But I don't love thee in office
   So I won't give you my vote.

JUNO
The Nude Frontier

The television debates between Richard M. Nixon and John F. Kennedy were clearly the most important factor in establishing Kennedy as a serious contender for the presidency. They reversed his standing in the polls from underdog to the leading candidate and wiped out once and for all the accusations that he was too young, too inexperienced for the top job. They probably won him the election. All this was not so clear on the night of the first debate, nor shortly thereafter.

Nixon, vice president for nearly eight years, who had shaken his fist at Khrushchev and been stoned by a mob in Venezuela, ran on his experience, calling Kennedy a callow youth applying for a man's job. Kennedy, although campaigning vigorously and with high purpose in asking for a new America, seemed to be plagued by the recurring issue of his religion. That was what everyone had heard about.

When invited by the networks to debate, he agreed instantly and he agreed to every rule of the debate or setting, without asking for changes. There were to be four debates, one in September and three in October, covering domestic and foreign policy issues.

On the night of the first Great Debate, Monday September 26, I was driving to Boston to document the Kennedy Foundation, which had been severely attacked in the previous summer's special congressional session. I tuned in the radio and therefore missed the visual impact of the young, calm, cool senator and the sweating, tense, haggard-looking vice president. But there was no doubt, from what came over the radio, that Kennedy was establishing himself as at least the equal, if not the superior, candidate for president of the United States. First to make the opening statement, he started, "I think the question before the American people is are we doing as much as we can do? . . . If we fail then freedom fails . . . I am not satisfied as an American with the progress that we are making . . . I want people in Latin America and Africa and Asia to start to look to America . . . what the President of the United States is doing not . . . Khrushchev . . . Can freedom be maintained under the most severe attack it has ever known? I think it can and . . . it depends on what we do here." And Nixon could only agree with these goals, respond to Kennedy's leadership, clarify, or quibble.

Most of the next day's papers on the whole called it a draw. "Both candidates measured up in a difficult test," *Christian Science Monitor.* "A decorous draw," said the *Miami Herald,* and the *Richmond Ledger* thought that Nixon had won. But this could be called only bad judgment. For the first time in the history of political campaigning, the candidates for the two major parties had exposed their views on live television, a historic occasion. Between 85 million and 120 million viewers had watched one or all four debates, and had certainly made decisions about the men they watched.

The rest of the debates were less crucial, only one issue seeming to arouse passions: defence of the islands of Quemoi and Matsu, off the coast of China, islands which most Americans had never heard of. A respected research firm finally gave Kennedy a score of 39 against Nixon's 23, but by this time we knew, because the affection of the crowds had grown almost daily since that first debate.

SARAH McCLENDON, *El Paso Times:* Mr. President, sir, will you tell us some of the big decisions that Mr. Nixon has participated in since you have been in the White House and he, as vice president, has been helping you?
THE PRESIDENT: Well, Miss McClendon, no one participates in the decisions. I don't see why people can't understand this.
Q: We understand that the power of decision is entirely yours, Mr. President. I just wondered if you could give us an example of a major idea of his that you had adopted in that role, as the decider and final —
THE PRESIDENT: If you gave me a week I might think of one. I don't remember.

"I think it's time America started moving again."
JOHN F. KENNEDY

Lee Radziwill, Jacqueline Kennedy, Robert Kennedy and Kenny O'Donnell watch the third debate on television at ABC in New York.

"I was there on the morning when the decision on Lebanon was made. I was there when Trieste was decided. I was there when the decisions on Iran, all these others that have kept the peace and kept it without surrender, and, my friends, this I know — that America at this time cannot afford to use the White House as a training ground to give experience to somebody at the expense of the United States of America."

RICHARD M. NIXON

"What Mr. Nixon doesn't understand is that the President of the United States, Mr. Eisenhower, is not the candidate. You've seen those elephants in the circus . . . you know how they travel around the circus, by grabbing the tail of the elephant in front of them. That was all right in 1952 and in 1956 . . . but now Mr. Nixon meets the people. The choice is not President Eisenhower; the choice is whether the people of this country want the leadership of Mr. Nixon . . ."

JOHN F. KENNEDY

From the first television debate

"I see no shadows of gloom or doubt falling across this land. The twilight of America's promise is not near. No, this is the high noon of America — the high noon of responsibility for this generation of Americans."
LYNDON B. JOHNSON

Left, top to bottom: As the campaign crowds grew to near unmanageable proportions, a strange phenomenon developed. Young girls in the crowd would either stand in total silence, crying and shaking, or they would scream and kick, the "Screamers and Jumpers" we called them. Elvis Presley might be expected to receive this kind of near sexual adulation, but it was unknown for a political figure.

"The two political parties in our history have always been divided, as Emerson said, into the party of hope and into the party of memory."

JOHN F. KENNEDY

"We Catholics believe that the first time you visit a Catholic church you could make three wishes and I used to joke with Jack about it — we were in Anchorage, Alaska and we had never been in this church, the Holy Family Church in Anchorage. We were walking down the aisle and I said, 'Jack don't forget the three wishes,' and as he genuflected and looked toward the altar, I heard him whisper, 'New York, Pennsylvania and Texas.' "

DAVID F. POWERS

"Courage — not complacency — is our need today. Leadership — not salesmanship. And the only valid test of leadership is the ability to lead. Our ends will not be won by rhetoric. We can have faith in the future only if we have faith in ourselves."

JOHN F. KENNEDY

"I cannot assure you that the road ahead is an easy one — because I know it will not be easy, and our journey will require effort and sacrifice. But I believe that the people of this state — and the people of all America — can again begin its forward march. For I believe that we all share the faith of a great son of North Carolina, Thomas Wolfe, when he wrote:
I think the true discovery of America is before us. I think the true fulfillment of our spirit, of our people, of our might and immortal land, is yet to come."

JOHN F. KENNEDY

DAY IN LIMBO

An Uncertain Election Night

Kennedy arrives in Boston the day before the election.

" 'I know there is a God, and I know He hates injustice. I see the storm coming and I know His hand is in it. But if He has a place and a part for me, I believe that I am ready.' Now, a hundred years later, when the issue is still freedom or slavery, we know there is a God, and we know He hates injustice. We see the storm coming, and we know His hand is in it. But if He has a place and a part for me, I believe that we are ready. Thank you."

John F. Kennedy, quoting from a letter Abraham Lincoln wrote to a friend, at one of his last campaign appearances in Waterbury, Connecticut. After a long day, he had arrived in the town at 3 a.m. and an estimated 30,000 people were still waiting for him, yelling "We love you, Jack, we love you, Jack," and he spoke and came back again and again, until nearly four o'clock in the morning.

Robert Kennedy and Ethel voting in Hyannis Port.

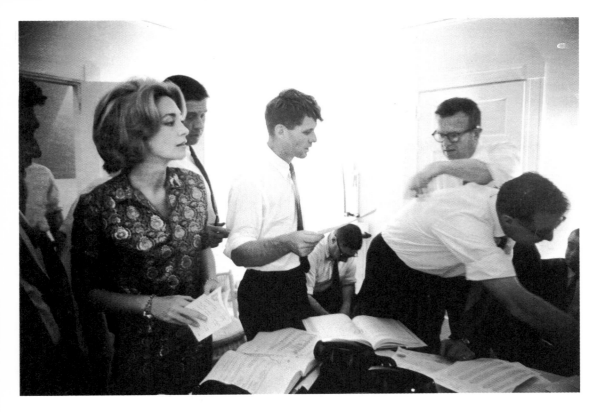

Family and staff worked feverishly through the night at several posts set up at Robert Kennedy's house at Hyannis Port.

The candidate remained in seclusion for most of that evening at his own house. As soon as darkness had fallen, TV networks had set up their lights, illuminating the house now, giving the effect of an empty movie set. Inside we could see the lights burning in the living room, and every once in a while the Senator would walk across the lawn to visit his brother Bobby's house. At around midnight he walked across once more, to remain for the rest of the night.

The command post had been set up on the second floor of Bobby's house, his children's bedrooms, now cleared of furniture. Outside a tickertape was clicking out results precinct by precinct. Below, on the sun porch, more than thirty direct telephone lines were in touch with crucial districts throughout the country, manned by the veterans of this cohesive team. Kennedys and campaign workers were rushing about, rumours and facts changed the mood constantly during the night and from time to time the candidate, almost inhumanly cool, would come in and receive an up-to-date report, almost impassively. The candidate went to sleep at 4 a.m. and so did I, on a cot in the maid's quarters, only to be woken up twice by false cries of, "He has conceded, he has conceded."

From left, Steve and Jean Smith, Pat, Rose Kennedy and Ethel, Teddy, Joan, Bobby and Lem Billings.

In the early hours of Wednesday November 9, the entire family went out for a long walk along the beach. Normally, by this time, the loser would have conceded and the new president would have been proclaimed, but this election was so close that there was still a chance, though remote, of defeat. Getting back to the house, a football game momentarily relaxed everyone, before they once more manned the phones and watched their own show on television.

"That's my brother Jack. All guts, no orains."
ROBERT F. KENNEDY, the morning after election day, in the football game, with the President-to-be fumbling the ball

By 10.30 a.m. the lead, which had stood at 2,300,000 shortly after midnight, was now reducing rapidly. Several states were in doubt and a worried family gathered at the stairwell of Joseph P. Kennedy's house. From left: Pat, a friend, Senator Kennedy, Teddy, Joseph P. Kennedy and Lem Billings.

From left to right in front of the television set. Pauline Fluet, secretary to Steve Smith, (standing), Eunice Shriver, Bill Walton, Pierre Salinger, the family chauffeur (on the stairs), Ethel and Robert Kennedy, Senator Kennedy and Angie Novello, secretary to Robert Kennedy.

On election night one of the network's computers had gone awry. Taking all voting information into account, the computer had predicted a landslide victory for Nixon; he was to be a 100-to-1 winner and carry 459 electoral votes against Kennedy's 78. Moreover, John Chancellor, a respected NBC commentator, had predicted a Nixon sweep. All of that had been dismissed by 11 a.m. the morning after election day, but the early 2 million plus lead had been whittled down to almost 100,000 and Illinois was still out. It took that state's leading Democrat, Mayor Richard Daley of Chicago, to pronounce Kennedy the winner and take us over the top. The votes produced by Daley were in fact challenged but the matter was not pursued when Nixon dropped his threatened legal challenge, largely because votes in Republican down-state Illinois were also considered dubious.

"I am sure that many are listening here who supported Mr. — Senator Kennedy. I know too that he probably is listening to this program. And while the — please, please, just a minute . . . while there are still some results yet to come — if the trend continues, Mr. — Senator Kennedy will be the next President of the United States."

RICHARD M. NIXON
conceding the election

"You know that election night, we're all at Bobby's, you recall, it's 3.30 and we're frozen at 241 — we're leading in Illinois, Michigan, and a few other places, but he wanted to go over to be where Jackie and Caroline were — so we're walking through the darkness over to his house . . . and I said, 'How could you go to bed now?' — we've crisscrossed the country for four years now and what a great answer — he said, 'It's too late to change another vote, and I need some sleep.' "

DAVID F. POWERS

Minutes before the final election
victory, the family confers on the porch
of Robert Kennedy's house.

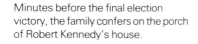

Moments after the triumph.

The President-Elect meeting his Secret Service men for the first time.

It was astonishing. As the frontrunner's large margin was being chipped away, the Secret Service had installed two teams of sixteen agents each in Los Angeles, where Nixon was waiting for the results, and near the Kennedy compound in Hyannis Port. By 7 a.m. the East Coast group had received the nod and were in place. Everyone on the compound and those coming from outside were known to them, their functions established. They addressed us all by name.

"Jacqueline Kennedy described the period between the closing of the polls and the moment of victory as 'the longest night in history'. Now she seemed dazed as people rushed up to congratulate her. After a while, she donned her raincoat and went for a solitary walk along the beach. In Bobby's living room the scene had changed remarkably. Finally there was certainty, and the long struggle was over. A sigh of relief was almost audible, and all got up and walked into the sun room, where they stood with bright smiles, looking up at their brother. Then John Kennedy asked for his wife, and he went down to the beach to find her. While Jacqueline went in to dress for a picture and get ready to go to the Armory, John F. Kennedy went for a long walk with Caroline."

JACQUES LOWE

"Good morning, Mr. President."
CAROLINE KENNEDY to her father on election morning

The President went for a walk with Caroline. I went with him, trailed by agents. Then it was on to the Hyannis Armory to meet the world's press.

"So now my wife and I prepare for a new administration, and for a new baby."
JOHN F. KENNEDY

Shortly after victory finally came, following the long night and morning, the entire family was due to appear at the Hyannis Armory, where the world's press had been waiting for hours. The family, still in casual dress, had to get ready. I knew that never again would they all be together and I knew that I had something like twenty minutes to convince everyone that a family photograph had to be taken on this unique historic occasion, and then to take the photograph as well. No one's mind was on photographs, everyone said "after", an after that I knew would never happen. I rushed around obsessed, knocking on doors, pleading, and finally the patriarch, Joseph P. Kennedy, decided that indeed the photograph would have to be taken.

By that time two other photographers, who had been with us during the entire campaign, Paul Schutzer of *LIFE* and Stanley Tretick of UPI, were invited in to participate in the event. When the First-Lady-to-be arrived at the door, Senator Kennedy went over and took her by the arm, a gallant gesture, and the entire family rose and applauded. A moving moment indeed. Then there were five minutes left to complete the task. It was sheer bedlam, with three photographers trying to get attention and shouting instructions, "Turn left, move right, Mr. Kennedy Senior, please lean forward . . ." and the sitters having no idea where to look, what to do, whether to be serious or smile.

From left, seated: Eunice Kennedy Shriver, Rose Fitzgerald Kennedy, Joseph P. Kennedy, Jacqueline Bouvier Kennedy, Edward M. Kennedy, Sargent Shriver. *Standing :* Ethel Skakel Kennedy, Stephen Smith, Jean Kennedy Smith, The President-Elect John F. Kennedy, Robert F. Kennedy, Patricia Kennedy Lawford, Joan Bennett Kennedy and Peter Lawford.

CAMELOT

Inauguration of the 35th President

On Inauguration morning, the President-Elect, returning from Mass, enters his Georgetown home for the last time.

Summoning artists to participate
In the august occasions of the state
Seems something artists ought to celebrate.
Today is for my cause a day of days.

We see how seriously the races swarm
In their attempts at sovereignty and form.
They are our wards we think to some extent
For the time being and with their consent,
To teach them how Democracy is meant.
"New order of the ages" did we say?
If it looks none too orderly today,
'Tis a confusion it was ours to start
So in it have to take courageous part.
No one of honest feeling would approve
A ruler who pretended not to love
A turbulence he had the better of.

Come fresh from an election like the last,
The greatest vote a people ever cast,
So close yet sure to be abided by,
It is no miracle our mood is high.
Courage is in the air in bracing whiffs
Better than all the stalemate ands and ifs.
There was the book of profile tales declaring
For the emboldened politicians daring
To break with followers when in the wrong,
A healthy independence of the throng,
A democratic form of right divine
To rule first answerable to high design.
There is a call to life a little sterner,
And braver for the earner, learner, yearner.
Less criticism of the field and court
And more preoccupation with the sport.
It makes the prophet in us all presage
The glory of a next Augustan age
Of a power leading from its strength and pride,
Of young ambition eager to be tried,
Firm in our free beliefs without dismay,
In any game the nations want to play.
A golden age of poetry and power
Of which this noonday's the beginning hour.

From *Gift Outright* of "The Gift Outright",
ROBERT FROST

At the Inaugural Ball.

Left, top and bottom: Sinatra staging the Gala spectacular.
Above: The President-Elect and Mrs. Kennedy arriving at the
Inaugural Gala. The President stayed until 3 a.m.

A law was made a distant moon ago here,
July and August cannot be too hot;
And there's a legal limit to the snow here
In Camelot . . .

The winter is forbidden till December
And exits March the second on the dot.
By order summer lingers through September
In Camelot . . .

The rain may never fall till after sundown.
By eight the morning fog must disappear
In short there's simply not
A more congenial spot . . .
Than Camelot . . .

I know it sounds a bit bizarre,
But in Camelot . . .
That's how conditions are.

"Camelot"
Words and music by
ALAN JAY LERNER and FREDERICK LOEWE

Gene Kelly, ''Singing in the Rain''.

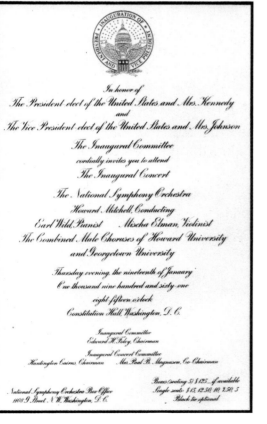

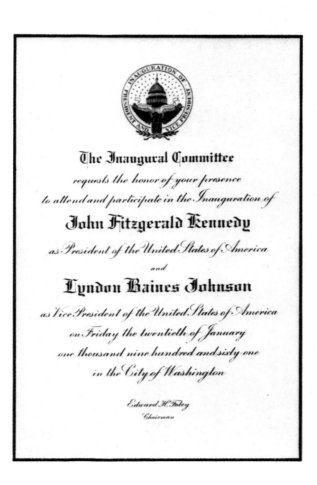

President Kennedy speaking at the Inaugural Ball.

Frank Sinatra entertains at the Inaugural Gala.

John F. Kennedy being sworn in by Chief Justice Earl Warren, who was later to head the controversial Warren Commission, which investigated the President's assassination — an investigation which raised more questions than it answered and satisfied no one. The date is January 20, 1961. Kennedy took the oath on his family's Bible.

"... Let the word go forth from this time and place, to friend and foe alike, that the torch has been passed to a new generation of Americans — born in this century, tempered by war, disciplined by a hard and bitter peace, proud of our ancient heritage ...

"Let every nation know, whether it wishes us well or ill, that we shall pay any price, bear any burden, meet any hardship, support any friend, oppose any foe to assure the survival and the success of liberty ...

"To those peoples in the huts and villages of half the globe, struggling to break the bonds of mass misery, we pledge our best efforts to help them help themselves ...

"So let us begin anew — remembering on both sides that civility is not a sign of weakness, and sincerity is always subject to proof. Let us never negotiate out of fear. But let us never fear to negotiate ...

"All this will not be finished in the first one hundred days. Nor will it be finished in the first one thousand days, nor in the life of this Administration, nor even perhaps in our lifetime on this planet. But let us begin ...

"Now the trumpet summons us again — not as a call to bear arms, though arms we need — not as a call to battle, though embattled we are — but a call to bear the burden of a long twilight struggle, year in and year out, 'rejoicing in hope, patient in tribulation' — a struggle against the common enemies of man: tyranny, poverty, disease and war itself ...

"And so, my fellow Americans: ask not what your country can do for you — ask what you can do for your country.

"My fellow citizens of the world: ask not what America will do for you, but what together we can do for the freedom of man."

JOHN F. KENNEDY
Inaugural Address, January 20, 1961

President and Mrs. Kennedy return from the swearing-in ceremony to the White House. The President, in spite of the freezing temperatures, used an open car, a matter which caused great concern to the Secret Service, the presidential bodyguard. This was the beginning of what was to become known as the "Kennedy Style"

The land was ours before we were the land's.
She was our land more than a hundred years
Before we were her people. She was ours
In Massachusetts, in Virginia,
But we were England's, still colonials,
Possessing what we still were unpossessed by,
Possessed by what we now no more possessed
Something we were withholding made us weak
Until we found out that it was ourselves
We were withholding from our land of living,
And forthwith found salvation in surrender.
Such as we were we gave ourselves outright
(The deed of gift was many deeds of war)
To the land vaguely realizing westward,
But still unstoried, artless, unenhanced,
Such as she was, such as she would become.

ROBERT FROST, "The Gift Outright"

The eighty-six-year-old poet had been unable to read the poem
especially composed for the Inauguration of President John F. Kennedy
because of the glaring sunlight. He recited instead "The Gift Outright"
from memory.

The Inauguration of any president is a great event,
bringing thousands of visitors to the capital to bask in the
reflection of their chosen leader. This one surpassed all
others. Out of power for eight years, the Democrats were
boisterous. Moreover Kennedy, the youngest president
since Teddy Roosevelt, had attracted a new generation to
his cause, men and women for whom this Inauguration
was their first, and they were determined to celebrate.
They came from every state of the Union, by car, by
plane, by train, bringing their evening clothes, ready to
stay awake for the three days of the inaugural festivities.
Hotel rooms were considered bargains at five times their
normal price and many visitors slept in their cars.

The Inaugural Gala, the high point of the festivities, which
cost the revellers $100 a ticket was staged by Frank
Sinatra. It featured an extravaganza starring Gene Kelly,
Ella Fitzgerald, Ethel Merman, Tony Curtis, Janet Leigh,
Laurence Olivier, Frederic March, Harry Belafonte, Nat
King Cole and many others, and the orchestra was
conducted by Leonard Bernstein. But there were
problems. On Thursday morning, the day before the
Inauguration, a sudden blizzard hit Washington, covering
the capital with eight inches of snow in a few hours. All
traffic stopped and few celebrators were able to reach the
afternoon's events, let alone get to their hotels and
change into formal wear. I myself missed three
receptions and covered the black tie Inaugural Gala, from
the presidential box, in a bow tie and wearing a sports
jacket. It had taken more than four hours from the Armory
and back and I had been unable to change.

Vice President Johnson and President Kennedy watching the parade. On the right is Lady Bird Johnson.

President Kennedy and Vice President Johnson with Jacqueline Kennedy and Parade Grand Marshal Lt.General James M. Gavin, soon to be Ambassador to France, watching the parade from the presidential box.

The Inaugural Parade started at 2 p.m. and it was dark by the time it ended. There were 32,000 marchers, 86 bands (featuring drum majorettes frozen blue), the entire West Point Corps of Cadets and Annapolis Brigade of Midshipmen, jets, tanks, missiles, horses, mules and dogs. Every state of the Union provided a float, as did Puerto Rico, the Virgin Islands, Guam and American Samoa.

Right, top to bottom: Sam Rayburn, ''Mr. Speaker'', ex-President Harry Truman, and Supreme Court Justice Felix Frankfurter, watching as guests of the President.

The President, staying to the bitter end and hatless most of the time, enjoyed himself immensely. When float PT 109 came by with his wartime crew atop, a roar went forth from the distinguished gathering. Having invited me into his box, the President asked how it was going, was I getting my photographs, did I need anything. He then called me over again, wondering whether I was enjoying myself. I had never seen him so jovial, so totally relaxed. As night fell the President went "home" to the White House and on to the Inaugural Ball, where he stayed until 3 a.m. He had called a staff meeting for 9 the next morning. The New Frontier was about to begin.

"Are you getting any good shots, Jacques?"
"Yes, Mr. President."

The Inaugural Ball, seen from the presidential box.

"*I think this is an ideal way to spend an evening — you looking at us and we looking at you.*"
JOHN F. KENNEDY

Jacqueline Kennedy, Robert and Teddy Kennedy at the Inaugural Ball.

THE THOUSAND DAYS

The Bay of Pigs · The Race to the Moon · Steel Crisis · Civil Rights ·
The Beginnings of Vietnam · The Cuban Missile Crisis ·
Attorney General Robert F. Kennedy

President John Fitzgerald Kennedy in his office at the White House.

It was on Saturday January 21, 1961 that the new administration began. President Kennedy entered the Oval Office at ten minutes to nine and his staff was in place by nine o'clock. The walls of his office were bare and painted a putrid green, and the parquet floor still bore the marks of the cleats on Eisenhower's golf shoes. The President's first act was to place pictures of his family on his desk and order the office repainted an off-white colour. Later it would become a warm and very personal room, with pictures of sailing ships on the wall, the famous coconut on the desk, and his own books, handsomely bound in leather, on the shelves. His wife would find a desk in the White House basement, a gift of Queen Victoria to Rutherford B. Hayes in 1878, made from the timber of HMS *Resolute*.

Kennedy's first visitor that day was ex-President Harry Truman, who at first had opposed him and then berated those who voted against him in colourful language. Mayor Richard Daley came by with his six children and so did Robert Frost. Both the Cabinet and the White House staff were sworn in that day. The new President sent greetings to the leaders of the Soviet Union and he thanked the Democratic National Committee for their work, mentioning the $4 million debt the Democrats had run up. It was a calm day, but the calm wasn't to last.

This was to be a different administration from any of its predecessors. This President would be highly accessible and active. In the electronic age he would open his press conferences to live television. Impatient, he would often dial his own calls, to the consternation of the recipients, including me. He would set new styles, reach out to the arts and men of letters and demand excellence and dedication from all who worked for him.

His true concerns became clear in the first few days. Shocked ever since the West Virginia primary to see the true extent of poverty in America, his first Executive Orders were to double the food rations for the needy at home and to strengthen the Food for Peace programme abroad. Urban renewal, extension of unemployment benefits, aid to needy children, the Minimum Wage Bill, health insurance for the aged, and, his most cherished programme, the Peace Corps, came shortly after, bringing to life his inaugural exhortation: "Do not ask what your country can do for you, but ask what you can do for your country."

He wanted a man on the moon, if possible an American, and his dream was a world at peace and without hunger, with civil rights at home and abroad, the preservation of democracy and liberty for all. It wouldn't all work out quite that way, and he knew it, but he agreed with the Chinese proverb that, "A journey of a thousand miles begins with one step."

"Winston Churchill once said that democracy is the worst form of government except for all the other systems that have been tried. It is the most difficult. It requires more of you — discipline, character, self-restraint, a willingness to serve the public interest . . . and unless in this free country of ours we are able to demonstrate that we are able to make this society work and progress, unless we can hope that from you we are going to get back all of the talents which society has helped develop in you, then, quite obviously, all the hopes of all of us that freedom will not only endure but prevail . . . will be disappointed."
JOHN F. KENNEDY

I am Liberty — God's daughter!
My symbols — a law and a torch;
Not a sword to threaten slaughter,
Nor a flame to dazzle or scorch;
But a light that the world may see
And a truth that shall make men free.
JOHN BOYLE O'REILLY, "Liberty Lighting the World"

The Staff

The President with Kenny O'Donnell.

"Good morning, Mr. President."
"Good morning, Mr. Ambassador."

Kennedy and Dave Powers greeting each other on the first day in the White House

The President's relations with his staff were relaxed and easy. Although expected to work long hours and live up to a code of excellence rarely before demanded, it was a happy White House, full of good humour. The President read Salinger's press briefings every day, both for information and "for their entertainment value", for the corpulent Press Secretary often came in for severe ribbing. When the President had announced a fitness programme that included a fifty-mile hike for the White House staff and the press asked Pierre whether he would participate, his answer was, "I might be plucky, but I am not stupid," and on the same issue the President presented Dave Powers with a fifty-mile hike certificate "for hiking to my ice-box to drink up all my Heinekens". Powers, his oldest political friend, was the President's closest companion during the White House years, outside the family. Every day they would swim together in the White House pool and Dave would keep him company in the private quarters when Mrs. Kennedy and the children were out of Washington. They would share a simple meal and watch some television or the President would read a book while Dave would drink his Heinekens. Around eleven o'clock on a normal day the President would go to bed. Dave would watch him kneel to say his prayers, see him get into bed, turn off the lights and drive home.

The staff was divided into factions. The Irish mafia included Appointments Secretary Kenneth O'Donnell, Congressional Relations chief Lawrence O'Brien, and Dave Powers, intimate and devoted friends, dating back to the early political wars. A second group, the egg-heads, were led by Theodore Sorensen, who had joined Kennedy in his Senate office and become his premier speech-writer, and included Richard Goodwin and Arthur Schlesinger Jr. The two groups, the first pragmatic and the second intellectual, rarely agreed and were often at loggerheads. A third group included everyone else.

But the staff was kept relatively small. Richard Neustadt, an expert on presidential power and how to use it, an adviser during and just after the transition (but who had refused an appointment), had carefully limited the use of White House stationery to a chosen few.

The President with David Bell, the Director of the Budget (centre), and Ted Sorensen, Special Assistant.

The President with Richard Goodwin, speech-writer and member of the White House staff.

The Cabinet

President Kennedy at a Cabinet meeting.

"*Although President Kennedy is very popular, he has not yet been able to carry the country with him. He has not yet won over the minds of the people. This may be because he has not yet conquered their hearts by opening his own.*"

WALTER LIPPMAN
Newsweek

"*It is a good thing to have a brave man as our President in times as tough as these are for our country and the world.*"

ERNEST HEMINGWAY
In a letter to the President

Walter Heller, Chairman of the Council of Economic Advisers, reports to the Cabinet. On the President's right, a place of honour, always sits the senior member, the Secretary of State, here Dean Rusk, followed by the Attorney General, Robert Kennedy, Secretary of Commerce Luther Hodges, Secretary of Health, Education and Welfare Abraham Ribicoff, Secretary of Labor Arthur Goldberg, Secretary of Defense Robert McNamara, the Vice President (who always sits opposite the President), Lyndon Johnson, and Postmaster General (a Cabinet post since abandoned) Edward Day. On the President's left are Secretary of the Treasury Douglas Dillon and Secretary of the Interior Stewart Udall. In the background are White House aides Ted Sorensen and Fred Dutton. Normally the Secretary of State is the most powerful Cabinet figure, but in this administration the Attorney General and the Secretary of Defense were the strong figures. The post of the Ambassador to the United Nations had also been elevated to Cabinet level, but Adlai Stevenson, busy in New York, did not attend many Cabinet meetings. Secretary of Agriculture Orville Freeman was also absent from this meeting. He normally sat between the Secretaries of Defense and Labor.

It was an unusual Cabinet. One member, Douglas Dillon, was a Republican and a large contributor to Nixon's campaign funds. The President had never met McNamara and Rusk until after his election. Edward Day had been a Stevenson supporter. Only two men were long-time supporters of the President, his own brother and Abe Ribicoff. Two of the members were Jewish and no attempt had been made to draft Catholics. But the President had won the election owing no political debt to anyone and the members of his administration were to be chosen on ability alone. His style, moreover, was not much suited to government by consensus. He felt that the President alone carried the final burden and, though listening to all the advice he could get, made the final decision. He loved to recount the story of Abraham Lincoln asking his Cabinet, "All in favor say 'aye' " and the whole Cabinet voting "aye", followed by "All opposed say 'no' " and Lincoln voting "no", then declaring the vote to be "no".

I worked with the President many nights. He would be alone except for me; dictating letters, reading correspondence, doing paperwork until late into the night. His most disconcerting habit was to pick up the telephone, bypassing the White House switchboard, and call people directly, apparently without realizing what a direct call from the President meant to them. One particular night I remember well. He called the distinguished editor of the *Atlanta Constitution*, Ralph McGill, wanting him to serve on a committee. His young daughter answered, wanting to know who was calling, so that she could tell "mommy". He said, the President. The ensuing conversation between the President of the United States and the little girl was hilarious beyond belief. Here was the most powerful man in the Western world explaining to a five- or six-year-old (I never did find out her age) that he wanted to speak to her daddy and that he was the President of the United States of America. A startled Mrs. McGill finally came on the telephone, promising her husband's return call. I myself received many such calls.

Congress

Congressional breakfast meeting at the White House. From left, Speaker of the House Rayburn, the President and Senate Majority Leader Mansfield. Labor Secretary Goldberg and Press Secretary Salinger attended as observers. With their backs to the camera, House Majority Leader McCormack and Vice President Johnson.

"The election in 1960 was very close. It has meant that nearly every vote in the House and Senate is close. Some we win by one or two votes; others we lose."

JOHN F. KENNEDY on the defeat of his Medicare bill, July 17, 1962

President Kennedy with Congressional Relations Chief Larry O'Brien and Vice President Johnson. Behind them, a reporter. The Vice President presides over the Senate, and in the case of a deadlock may cast the deciding vote.

In the fulfilment of President Kennedy's vision for the country and the world, Congress proved to be the most obstinate stumbling block. It was dominated for years by a conservative coalition of Southern Democrats and Republicans. These long-entrenched, powerful old men looked with suspicion on this young, liberal President and his progressive plans. For years they had blocked forward-looking legislation, especially in the fields of civil rights, aid to the poor, minimum wages and labour issues. Now this President, it was already clear, not only wanted to move forward in these known areas, but was adding such unacceptable reforms as medical aid for the elderly at home and an accelerated foreign-aid programme abroad. Moreover, the President's paper-thin election margin had not helped Democrats generally and some twenty-nine pro-Kennedy congressmen had gone down to defeat. The Senate, though not as cumbersome a body, was not much more co-operative.

The President was fully aware of his dilemma, and, from the beginning used every means at his disposal — press conferences, speeches around the country, television addresses — to energize the nation behind his programmes and force Congress to pass his bills. And he wooed the legislators themselves by such means as remembering their birthdays, inviting them to White House dinners and receptions, and by direct telephone calls. He also bypassed them at times, using the Executive Order, which needed no legislative consent, and other means.

In the end an uneasy relationship developed between the White House and Capitol Hill, and out of the 1054 requests Kennedy sent to Congress in his barely three years in office, an important number of progressive bills were passed. But it would be up to Lyndon Johnson with his phenomenal election victory over the Republicans to complete the Kennedy programme.

"In politics you have no friends, only allies."

JOHN F. KENNEDY

The Bay of Pigs

The invasion of Cuba, to become known as the Bay of Pigs, was the President's first major setback in office; in fact it was probably the first total defeat of the forty-three-year-old President's life. Many of his old friends said that they had never seen him so distraught and that "he was close to crying".

The operation had started a year before John F. Kennedy entered the White House. The brainchild of the CIA and specifically the agency's DDP (Deputy Director for Plans) Richard Bissell, it had been cloaked in such secrecy that no one but Bissell and his boss, CIA director Allen Dulles, knew what was really going on. President Eisenhower was doubtful about the invasion plans. Still, at the transition meeting on January 19 in the White House the old general told the young President-to-be that the operation was going well and that it was the new administration's "responsibility" to do "whatever is necessary" to bring it to a successful conclusion.

Kennedy had stumbled into the affair unwittingly during the fourth television debate with Richard Nixon. One of his speech-writers, Richard Goodwin, a coiner of elegant phrases, had written a routine press release: "We must attempt to strengthen the non-Batista democratic anti-Castro forces in exile, and in Cuba itself, who offer eventual hope of overthrowing Castro. Thus far, these fighters for freedom have had virtually no support from our government." He tried to have Kennedy approve the statement, but the candidate was dead tired and asleep at his hotel, and since the statement was routine, it was handed to the press. The *New York Times* headlined the story: "Kennedy Asks Aid for Cuban Rebels to Defeat Castro, Urges Support of Exiles and 'Fighters for Freedom' ".

Nixon, who knew of the clandestine operation and wanted it to happen prior to the election, was livid as he thought Kennedy also knew, and during the debate he attacked Kennedy, saying that it was "the most shockingly reckless proposal ever made . . . by a presidential candidate", and he went on to predict, almost prophetically, what eventually did happen, defeat and world

Q. Mr. President, has a decision been reached on how far this country will be willing to go in helping an anti-Castro uprising or invasion of Cuba?
THE PRESIDENT: . . . I want to say that there will not be, under any conditions, an intervention in Cuba by the United States Armed Forces. This government will do everything it possibly can, and I think it can meet its responsibilities, to make sure that there are no Americans involved in any actions inside Cuba.

Press Conference, April 12, 1961

Left: President Kennedy meeting with his Joint Chiefs of Staff. The Bay of Pigs is on the agenda. From left, General Thomas D. White (Air Force), Admiral Arleigh ''Thirty-Knot'' Burke (Navy), General George H. Decker (Army) and the Chairman, General Lyman Lemnitzer. The Joint Chiefs had appointed a committee to study in general terms what might be done to unseat Castro, and they had produced a ''white paper'', outlining six approaches to the dilemma for the President's consideration. The chiefs had been ordered to review the CIA plan for the first time in January 1961, but they were to ''advise'' only and not to ''become involved''. Their enthusiasm for the plan had never been strong, their briefings by the CIA had always been scanty and the chiefs believed that without full US naval support and guaranteed air supremacy there would be only a thirty-per-cent chance of success. Most of the chiefs had strong doubts about the final invasion plans, but they never voiced them forcefully to the President.

The military meeting again, now joined by Walt W. Rostow (third from left), General David Shoup speaking to Rostow, and General Andrew J. Goodpaster next to Admiral Burke.

Richard Bissell (rear), Allen Dulles (centre), McGeorge Bundy (centre right) and others, attending a National Security Council meeting.

condemnation. The President-Elect was finally briefed on November 27 by Bissell and Dulles. Kennedy was concerned at the scope of the operation, although that scope in terms of men was never great. The operation itself had been a disaster almost from the beginning.

The agency had tried to assassinate Castro, making contact with the underworld who had formerly operated Havana's casinos. Poisoned cigars to be handed to the Cuban dictator were among several attempts, none of which came off.

The Cuban fighters themselves, under uneasy American command, argued constantly and at one point went on strike. The secrecy surrounding the operation, with no one really knowing even his own duties, resulted in total confusion. Above all the operation was based on wishful thinking, namely that once the 1500 or so men and (in the end) six planes had landed, up to one-quarter of the population would rise up in revolt.

President Kennedy throughout was wary of the entire effort. He kept open his option to cancel the operation up to the last moment. He listened to voices of dissent from people who were concerned with the legality of the United States attacking a small country and with world opinion. He insisted that no Americans would be involved, on the ground, in the air or on the high seas, a decision which probably doomed the entire operation. But in the end the sheer momentum was too much, and he approved an operation shorn of real American support. When, at the critical moment of failure, it was time for the men to fade into the mountains and start a planned guerilla action, he found to his horror that there were no mountains, only swamps. Castro took 1189 men prisoner, whom he eventually exchanged for a ransom of food and drugs worth 53 million dollars.

The New Frontier, that group of vigorous, decisive brilliant men who had little regard for the studied ways of the Eisenhower or Truman days, had been dealt a severe blow. From then on the new President would be more careful, more questioning, more reflective of power and how to use it. He would come out of this intact, a better President.

"This participation of the United States in the aggression against Cuba was dramatically proved this morning when our antiaircraft batteries brought down a US military plane piloted by a US airman who was bombing the civilian population and our infantry forces in the area of Australia Central."

Radio Havana, official government communiqué No. 3

Fidel Castro at the Bay of Pigs.

President Kennedy in conversation with Secretary Rusk and CIA DDP Richard Bissell after a meeting about Cuba.

"There is an old saying that victory has a hundred fathers and defeat is an orphan. I am the responsible officer of the government."

JOHN F. KENNEDY

A high-level meeting about Cuba is about to start. From left: General Chester V. "Ted" Clifton, the President's military aide, Secretary of Defense McNamara, Chairman of the Joint Chiefs of Staff General Lyman Lemnitzer, CIA Director Allen Dulles, Deputy Director for Plans Richard Bissell, who masterminded the fiasco, and Walt W. Rostow, deputy to McGeorge Bundy (hidden left), the President's National Security Adviser.

"All my life I've known better than to depend on the experts. How could I've been so stupid to let them go ahead?"

JOHN F. KENNEDY

Attorney General Robert F. Kennedy

Attorney General Robert F. Kennedy in his office at the Justice Department, during a meeting with a group of political malefactors. The steely eyes, when challenged, were to become famous.

"I remember Bobby's extreme reluctance to be a member of the Cabinet. Yes. And I remember Jack's tremendous power of persuasion — I think it was one of the hardest things he really had to do was to overcome Bobby's reluctance."
ETHEL KENNEDY

Robert Kennedy confronts J. Edgar Hoover, FBI Director.

*"I think his attempt to bring the FBI under control and to have
a greater emphasis on white collar crime and organized crime
was positive. And on the other hand he supported the
appointment of some miserable racist to the Federal Appeals
court in the South and he was occasionally insensitive to civil
liberties."*

JACK NEWFIELD

*"To many his worst civil rights offence was his decision in
1963 to authorize J. Edgar Hoover to place a federal tap on the
phone of the civil rights leader Martin Luther King."*

BBC

*"The problem was that it now appears to be outrageous. But it
did not at the time (when) a very secret Communist member
very high up in the Communist Party was influencing Dr. King,
and those were the grounds that Mr. Hoover gave for doing it,
he circulated that information widely in the government and it
was rightly or wrongly Mr. Kennedy's judgment that the best
way of disproving any influence of that kind was to allow him
to put on the tap and not have all those other facts leak out and
destroy Dr. King by innuendo."*

NICHOLAS KATZENBACH

When John F. Kennedy appointed his brother Robert Attorney General an outcry rose from Democrats and Republicans alike. Southerners, especially, worried about an activist Attorney General confronting the civil rights problems, were concerned (and, as it turned out, had reason to be). The *New York Times* editorialized: "If Robert Kennedy was one of the outstanding lawyers of the country, a pre-eminent legal philosopher, a noted prosecutor . . . the situation would have been different . . ." The *New Republic* called him "not fit for the office". President Kennedy himself, when asked how he planned to announce the appointment, said jestingly, "Well, I think I'll open the front door of the Georgetown house some morning about 2 a.m., look up and down the street, and, if there's no one there, I'll whisper, it's Bobby."

But the decision to make the appointment or accept it had not been an easy one for the two brothers. Robert Kennedy was uncertain what he wished to do, torn between starting his own political career or joining the government in a less exposed position. He had actually turned the offer down. But the President insisted. He wanted Bobby in the government. He needed someone who would tell him the absolute truth, even when it hurt, which he knew was difficult for a President to get. Moreover, he needed him in the Cabinet, where he had few intimates. Above all, because of their relationship, Robert would be the second most powerful person in the government, a fact which ruled out any secondary position. Finally, he wanted him at Justice because he knew that the great domestic battles would be fought there, especially civil rights.

Bobby finally accepted and it turned out to be an inspired appointment. Robert F. Kennedy was to become one of the finest Attorney Generals in known memory. Backed by a brilliant staff, he came to assist his brother in all areas of government, often disagreeing, but often a crucial and tempering influence, as would be seen in the Cuban missile crisis.

"I came to this department ten years ago as an assistant attorney making $4200 a year. But I had ability and integrity, an interest in my work. I stayed late hours, my brother became President and now I am Attorney General . . . those qualifications are not necessarily listed in their order of importance."
ROBERT F. KENNEDY to Justice Department employees

The Attorney General, usually in shirtsleeves, worked and lunched at his desk. His normal day was twelve hours, more if a crisis arose. But the atmosphere, in spite of the exacting standards of performance he set, was jovial and relaxed. Many a high-level conference took place with the conferees standing around the desk, tossing a football across to each other from time to time. The forbiddingly dark, panelled walls of his office were lined with bright drawings by his children and dozens of artefacts, including a stuffed tiger, making the railroad-station-like vast chamber look almost gay. At weekends several children would be in attendance, with his favourite dog, a lumbering great animal called Brumus. The place would come alive.

"Damn it Bobby, comb your hair" and then *"Don't smile too much or they'll think we are happy about the appointment."*
JOHN F. KENNEDY to his brother before announcing the appointment to a critical press

"When Jack was elected and was forming his Cabinet, Bobby came to see me. Jack wanted him to be Attorney General, and Bobby wondered what he should do. Up to then he had had no real important bridge to cross . . . so he had quite a decision to make: whether to continue to sit in the shadow of his brother, would he be criticized? would it be harmful to his brother? would he make a good Attorney General? would it help or hurt his future? These are the kinds of things he talked about . . . He made I thought a very outstanding Attorney General."
WILLIAM O. DOUGLAS, Supreme Court Justice

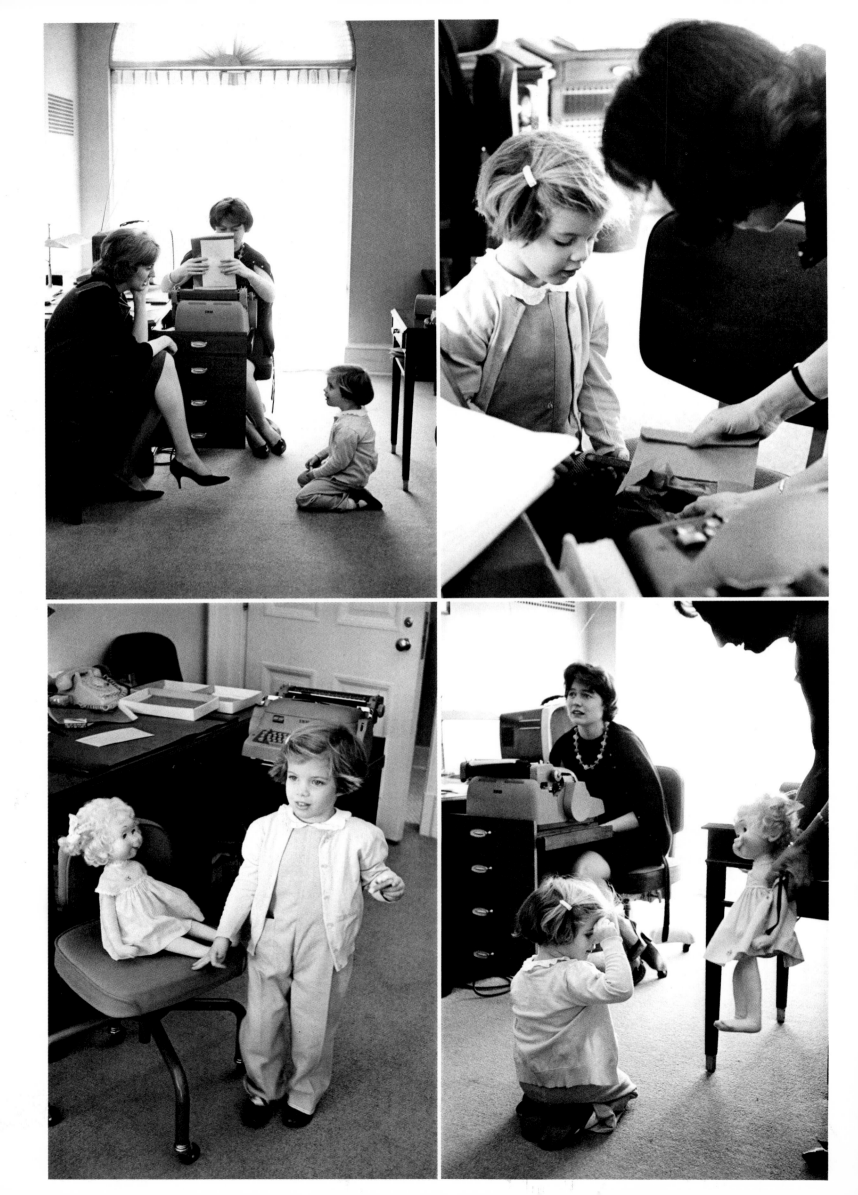

One addition to the normal staff of the White House was young Caroline. She would come down from the family quarters, bringing her doll, and haunt the offices. At the same time Mrs. Kennedy, for understandable reasons, wanted to protect her from the curiosity of the world press, from photographers lurking with telephoto lenses, from personal publicity. But the President, of course, at times differed. He asked me to take some pictures of Caroline and give them to *Newsweek*, where Ben Bradlee, his good friend, was the Washington editor. I told him that I couldn't do that, pointing out his wife's rather final edict. He said that I should give the pictures to Ben without telling her, and . . . without mentioning his request. I pointed out that the pictures would be published, in a major magazine at that, and could hardly be kept a secret. "You'll think of something to say," said the President, "but do it."

"I am reading more and enjoying it less."
JOHN F. KENNEDY remarking on newspaper coverage of his administration

He was a speedreader and his absorption of whatever he read, whether technical reports or poetry, was remarkable. And his recall was total. Once during the hectic West Virginia primaries I had taken some photographs of the candidate with Appalachian miners. He had asked me to send a photograph to each of them. Weeks later, halfway across the country, he wanted to know whether it had been done. It had. At another time, during a late-night radio interview after a hard day's campaigning, he took exception to a slighting remark about General de Gaulle made by a disc jockey. Kennedy quoted verbatim from a biography of de Gaulle, which had only that week come into the bookstores. It was astonishing. We had been campaigning from early morning to after midnight every day. When had he read the book? And of course all his speeches were punctuated by favourite poems, or quotations of the men and women he admired.

" 'Jack . . . I just happened to pick up . . . a new . . . biography of President McKinley . . . Of course, you haven't read it.'

"He said, 'What do you mean, I haven't; of course I have.'

" 'Jack, now look here, this book only came out two or three months ago; when the hell did you ever have time to read that 600-page book?'

" 'Well,' he said, 'Mr. Luce, you've forgotten the kind of life I've been leading.'

" 'What do you mean?'

" 'Well, I spend all this time in airplanes.'

"To me this was amazing that the man in the middle of the terrific campaign he was in, the presidential nomination campaign, could have found time to read, among other books, a 600-page volume on McKinley. But the late President's intellectual interest in politics was well illustrated by that. I remember another occasion, in the White House upstairs . . . there were two or three children's books, which evidently the President had been reading to his children. There was a novel by Disraeli . . . the President evidently was reading . . . I doubt if there are more than half a dozen people in the United States who have read Disraeli's novels in the last decade, but the President was one of them."

HENRY R. LUCE

"I speak of peace because of the new face of war. Total war makes no sense... It makes no sense in an age when a single nuclear weapon contains almost ten times the explosive force delivered by all of the allied air forces in the Second World War. It makes no sense in an age when the deadly poisons produced by a nuclear exchange would be carried by wind and water and soil and seed to the far corners of the globe and to generations yet unborn...

"I speak of peace as the necessary rational end of rational men. I realize that the pursuit of peace is not as

conclusion that war is inevitable — that mankind is doomed — that we are gripped by forces we cannot control. We need not accept that view. Our problems are manmade — therefore, they can be solved by man...

"World peace ... does not require that each man love his neighbor — it requires only that they live together in mutual tolerance... History teaches us that enmities between nations... do not last forever. However fixed our likes and dislikes may seem, the tide of time and events will often bring surprising changes in the relations between nations and neighbors...

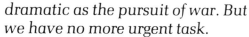

dramatic as the pursuit of war. But we have no more urgent task.

"Some say that it is useless to speak of world peace, of world law or world disarmament—and that it will be useless until the leaders of the Soviet Union adopt a more enlightened attitude. I hope they do. But I also believe that we must reexamine our own attitude — as individuals and as a nation — for our attitude is as essential as theirs ...

"Let us examine our attitude toward peace itself. Too many of us think it is impossible. Too many think it unreal. But that is a dangerous, defeatist belief. It leads to the

"Let us reexamine our attitude toward the Soviet Union. It is discouraging to think that their leaders may actually believe what their propagandists write..
"But it is also a warning—a warning to the American people not to fall into the same trap as the Soviets, not to see only a distorted and desperate view of the other side, not to see conflict as inevitable, accommodation as impossible, and communication as nothing more than an exchange of threats...

"It is an ironic but accurate fact that the two strongest powers are the two in the most danger of devastation. All we have built, all we have worked for, would be destroyed in the first twenty-four hours... for we are both devoting massive sums of money to weapons that could be better devoted to combating ignorance, poverty, and disease. We are both caught up in a vicious and dangerous cycle in which suspicion on one side breeds suspicion on the other, new weapons beget counter-weapons...

"So, let us not be blind to our differences — but let us also direct attention to our common interests and to the means by which those differences can be resolved. And if we cannot end now our differences, at least we can help make the world safe for diversity. For, in the final analysis, our most basic common link is that we all inhabit this small planet. We all breathe the same air. We all cherish our children's future. And we are all mortal...

"Above all, while defending our own vital interests, nuclear powers must avert those confrontations which bring an adversary to a choice of either a humiliating retreat or a nuclear war...

"At the same time we seek to keep peace inside the non-Communist world, where many nations, all of them our friends, are divided over issues which weaken Western unity, which invite Communist intervention or which threaten to erupt into war. Our efforts in West New Guinea, in the Congo, in the Middle East, and in the Indian sub-continent, have been persistent and patient despite criticism from both sides...

"The Communist drive to impose their political and economic system on others is the primary cause of world tension today. For there can be no doubt that, if all nations could refrain from interfering in the self-determination of others, the peace would be much more assured...

"Our primary long-range interest in Geneva is general and complete disarmament — designed to take place by stages, permitting parallel political developments to build the new institutions of peace which

would take the place of arms...

"To make clear our good faith and solemn convictions on the matter, I now declare that the United States does not propose to conduct nuclear tests in the atmosphere so long as other states do not do so...Such a declaration is no substitute for a formal binding treaty, but I hope it will help us achieve one. Nor would such a treaty be a substitute for disarmament, but I hope it will help us achieve it.

"Finally, my fellow Americans, let us examine our attitude toward peace and freedom here at home. The quality and spirit of our own society must justify and support our efforts abroad...we must all, in our daily lives, live up to the age-old faith that peace and freedom walk together. In too many of our cities today, the peace is not secure because freedom is incomplete...

"It is the responsibility of the executive branch at all levels of government...to provide and protect that freedom for all our citizens by all means within their authority. It is the responsibility of the legislative branch at all levels, wherever that authority is not now adequate, to make it adequate. And it is the responsibility of all citizens in all sections of this country to respect the rights of all others and to respect the law of the land.

" 'When a man's ways please the Lord,' the Scriptures tell us, 'he maketh even his enemies to be at peace with him.' And is not peace, in the last analysis, basically a matter of human rights — the right to live our lives without fear of devastation...

"The United States, as the world knows, will never start a war. We do not want a war...This generation of Americans has already had enough — more than enough — of war and hate and oppression...We shall do our part to build a world of peace where the weak are safe and the strong are just... Confident and unafraid, we labor on — not toward a strategy of annihilation but toward a strategy of peace."

JOHN F. KENNEDY
Address to the American University, Washington, June 10, 1963

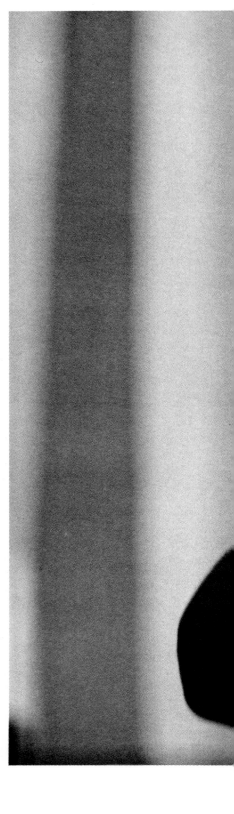

On February 13, 1961, United Nations Ambassador Adlai Stevenson came on the phone. I was alone with the President; his hand went to his head in utter despair, "Oh, no," I heard him groan. The Ambassador was informing the President of the assassination of Patrice Lumumba of the Congo, an African leader considered a trouble-maker and a leftist by many Americans. But Kennedy's attitude towards black Africa was that many who were considered leftists were in fact nationalists and patriots, anti-West because of years of colonialization, and lured to the siren call of Communism against their will. He felt that Africa presented an opportunity for the West, and, speaking as an American, unhindered by a colonial heritage, he had made friends in Africa and would succeed in gaining the trust of a great many African leaders. The call therefore left him heartbroken, for he knew that the murder would be a prelude to chaos in that mineral-rich and important African country. It was a poignant moment.

Later, returning from his meetings in Vienna with Khrushchev, the President would report to the American people that the Chairman had made one point with which he agreed, ". . . there are many disorders throughout the world, and he should not be blamed for all. He is quite right," said the President, and continued, "It is easy to dismiss as Communist-inspired every anti-government or anti-American riot, every overthrow of a corrupt regime, or every mass protest against misery and despair. These are not all Communist-inspired. The Communists move in to exploit them, to infiltrate their leadership, to ride their crest to victory. But the Communists did not create the conditions which caused them," and he went on to ask for an assistance programme for these nations in turmoil.

Kennedy and Macmillan on the lawn of the White House.

President Kennedy preferred to be his own Secretary of State and was in constant personal contact with the allied heads of state. A direct telephone link was established even with the Soviet Union, which served well in critical times. He enjoyed his relations with men of power, observed them, learned from them, and relaxed with them. He developed a particularly close relationship with Prime Minister Harold Macmillan, the wise elder statesman of British Tory politics. They considered each other friends. He admired General de Gaulle and that feeling was reciprocated. But Kennedy was deeply concerned as well with affairs in Africa, the Congo especially, and those in Southeast Asia. As a Senator he had made many statements on the war in Indochina and now Vietnam became again a matter of great concern to him.

"I think it might interest Your Majesty to have some impressions of the President on this, my fourth meeting with him. He was naturally suffering from the blow of his father's sudden illness, for the Kennedys are a devoted family. The President owes a great deal to his father and is obviously very attached to him. Moreover, it is a great shock to see a man perfectly fit one day and two days later struck down and permanently immobilized. I also thought the President's own health was not good. He is very restless owing to his back. He finds it difficult to sit in the same position for any length of time. I noticed the difficulty he had in picking up a piece of paper that had fallen on the floor. We produced a rocking chair, which was of some comfort to him. It is really rather sad that so young a man should be so afflicted, but he is very brave and does not show it except . . . by his unwillingness to continue to talk for any length of time without a break. He is also a very sensitive man, very easily pleased and very easily offended. He likes presents — I gave him one . . . He likes letters, he likes attention. To match this he is clearly a very effective, even ruthless, operator in the political field. I thought he was more interested in short-term — than in large and distant problems — but that is perhaps natural from his present experience. He is a most agreeable guest and carries the weight of his great office with simplicity and dignity . . ."

HAROLD MACMILLAN in a letter to Her Majesty the Queen of England, December 24, 1962

With the Danish Premier, Kampmann. *Below:* With Nkrumah of Ghana.

Steel Crisis

Robert Kennedy, Vice President Johnson and Secretary of Commerce Luther Hodges during the Steel Crisis. The President is in the background.

"In this serious hour in our nation's history, when we are confronted with grave crisis in Berlin and Southeast Asia, when we are devoting our energies to economic recovery and stability, when we are asking reservists to leave their homes and families for months on end and servicemen to risk their lives . . . and asking union members to hold down their wage requests at a time when restraint and sacrifice are being asked of every citizen, the American people will find it hard, as I do, to accept a situation in which a tiny handful of steel executives whose pursuit of private power and profit exceeds their sense of the public responsibility can show such utter contempt for the interests of 185 million Americans."

JOHN F. KENNEDY
Press Conference, April 11, 1962

"My father always told me that all businessmen were sons-of-bitches, but I never believed it till now."

JOHN F. KENNEDY according to the *New York Times*

The President later modified his father's statement, saying that generalizations are inaccurate and unfair and that, in any case, he had been talking about steelmen and in particular the 1937 strike. But he didn't deny the statement itself, remarking that he had found it appropriate that evening, that because the administration had not been "treated altogether with frankness", he thought his father's views had merit. "But that's past," he said, "now we are working together, I hope."

The Kennedy administration had been working hard to control inflation and for a year had urged the United Steelworkers of America, the union body, to come up with a non-inflationary wage package, which they had done, and the President and his Secretary of Labor congratulated themselves. Then only a week after the steel negotiations had been concluded, on April 10, 1962, US Steel, the largest producer, raised its prices by $6 a ton, to be followed by most of the other manufacturers in unison. The President was livid; he felt he had been double-crossed and the Office of the President offended. Instantly he sprang into action. Between his attending the annual Congressional Reception that night and welcoming the Shah of Iran the next day, the Department of Justice under Robert Kennedy started a grand jury investigation using the Sherman Antitrust Law, Senator Kefauver of the Senate Antitrust and Monopoly Subcommittee began an investigation, the Defense Department announced that it would shift its orders to companies holding the price line, and the wires between Washington and the steel companies were burning with intermediaries, in and out of government, trying to solve the crisis. And the President was in the thick of it, gaining forever the image of being anti-business. At his news conference the President spoke "with cold fury", calling the steel price rise an "irresponsible defiance of the public interest". But in seventy-two hours it was all over. The awesome power of the government had forced the companies to rethink their decision and they capitulated. The price came down.

Right, top: Discussing the crisis with Secretary of Labor Arthur Goldberg (centre) and President of the AFL–CIO George Meany. *Right, centre:* Later the President met Inland Steel Chairman Joseph L. Block (left), who was in Japan at the time of the crisis but refused to raise prices and thereby forced the other producers to rescind, and Tom Watson, Chairman of IBM (centre), at a regular scheduled meeting. The President was not "anti-business", he said. *Right:* The President with Walter Reuther of the United Automobile Workers.

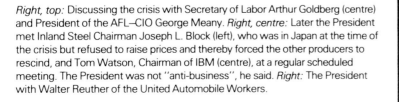

At the White House reception for Nobel prizewinners, the President and Jacqueline are flanked by the writer
Pearl S. Buck and Kennedy's favourite living poet, Robert Frost.

*"I think this is the most extraordinary collection of talent, of human knowledge, that has
ever been gathered together at the White House, with the possible exception of when
Thomas Jefferson dined alone . . .*

*"I know that every man here who has won the Nobel prize, not only does he build on the
past . . . on the efforts of other men and women, but he also builds on the efforts of those in
other countries; therefore . . . the Nobel prize has no national significance. But . . . we can
take some satisfaction that this hemisphere has been able to develop an atmosphere
which has permitted the happy pursuit of knowledge, and of peace; and that over forty
per cent of the Nobel prizes in the last thirty years have gone to men and women in this
hemisphere.*

*"And of particular pleasure today is the fact that thirteen Nobel prizes for peace have
gone to those who live in this hemisphere . . ."*

JOHN F. KENNEDY

"This will be the first speech about relations between France and the United States that does not include a tribute to General Lafayette . . . every Frenchman who comes to the United States . . . is astonished to find that we regard him as a golden, young romantic figure, next to George Washington our most distinguished citizen . . . I will mention a predecessor of mine, John Adams, who . . . asked that on his gravestone be written, 'He kept the peace with France.'

"I am very glad to welcome here some of our most distinguished artists. This is becoming a sort of eating place for artists. But they never ask us out!"

JOHN F. KENNEDY

"We believe that an artist, in order to be true to himself and his work, must be a free man or woman, and we are anxious to see emphasized the tremendous artistic talents we have available in this country.

"I don't think that even our fellow citizens are perhaps as aware as they should be of the hundreds of thousands of devoted musicians, painters, architects, those who work to bring about changes in our cities, whose talents are just as important a part of the United States as any of our perhaps more publicized accomplishments.

"So that we welcome you here to the White House — and most especially to welcome you, Maestro, and to tell you what a great honor it is to have you back in the White House."

JOHN F. KENNEDY

The First Lady in conversation with André Malraux at the reception in honour of the great writer and then French Minister for Culture.

Jacqueline Kennedy at a Congressional reception in the state dining room.

Pablo Casals is greeted by President Kennedy and Governor Munoz Marin of Puerto Rica after his recital. The venerable cellist had broken, for the first time, his vow never again to perform in a country which had supported Franco's Spain.

175

Civil Rights

James Howard Meredith, the first black to enter "Ole Miss", is here accompanied by Chief US Marshal James P. McShane (centre) and Justice Department Attorney John Doar (with his hand on Meredith's shoulder). They are refused permission to enter the campus of the University of Mississippi by Lieutenant Governor Paul Johnson.

"An unjust law is no law at all."
MARTIN LUTHER KING JR. quoting Saint Augustine

"In the absence of constitutional authority and without legislative action, an ambitious federal government, employing naked and arbitrary power, has decided to deny us the right of self-determination in the conduct of the affairs of our sovereign state.

"Even now as I speak to you tonight, professional agitators and the unfriendly liberal press and other trouble-makers are pouring across our borders intent upon instigating strife among our people.

"The Kennedy Administration is lending the power of the federal government to the ruthless demands of these agitators.

"I have made my position in this matter crystal clear. I have said in every county in Mississippi that no school in our state will be integrated while I am your Governor."
GOVERNOR ROSS BARNETT

"We didn't have much trouble with the freedom riders. When they didn't obey the officials here in the City of Jackson in Hinds County, we just simply put them in jail, and when the jails were all filled and the mayor's chicken coops down on the fairground were all filled, there were thirty-two of them left, and it was my happy privilege to send all of them to the State Penitentiary at Parchman and put them in maximum security cells. We put them in maximum security cells so they would be protected, you see. You haven't heard of any more freedom riders in Mississippi."
GOVERNOR ROSS BARNETT

"Those of us who are white can only dimly guess at what the pain of racial discrimination must be . . . How can a Negro father explain this intolerable situation to his children? And how can children be expected to grow up with any sense of pride in being Americans?"
ROBERT F. KENNEDY

Birmingham, Alabama.

"We preach freedom over the world, and we mean it, and we cherish our freedom here at home, but are we to say to the world and, much more importantly, to each other that this is a land of the free except for the Negroes; that we have no second-class citizens except Negroes; that we have no class or caste system, no ghettos, no master race except with respect to Negroes?"
JOHN F. KENNEDY

The Cuban Missile Crisis

"We had to establish a tangible and effective deterrent to American interference in the Caribbean. But what exactly? The logical answer was missiles...

"I found myself in the difficult position of having to decide on a course of action which would answer the American threat but which would also avoid war. Any fool can start a war, and once he's done so, even the wisest of men are helpless to stop it — especially if it's a nuclear war...

"My thinking went like this: if we installed the missiles secretly and then if the United States discovered the missiles were there after they were already poised and ready to strike, the Americans would think twice before trying to liquidate our installations by military means. I knew that the United States could knock out some of our installations, but not all of them. If a quarter or even a tenth of our missiles survived — even if only one or two big ones were left — we could still hit New York, and there wouldn't be much of New York left...

"While the Americans had no direct information about what we were delivering, they knew that whatever we were doing, we were doing with our own hands. It was not long before they concluded on the basis of reconnaissance photographs that we were installing missiles...

"The Americans became frightened, and we stepped up our shipments. We had delivered almost everything by the time the crisis reached the boiling point... we had installed enough missiles already to destroy New York, Chicago, and the other huge industrial cities, not to mention a little village like Washington. I don't think America had ever faced such a real threat of destruction as at that moment...

"I spent one of the most dangerous nights at the Council of Ministers office in the Kremlin. I slept on a couch in my office — and I kept my clothes on... I remember those days vividly...

"While we conducted some of this exchange through official diplomatic channels, the more confidential letters were relayed to us through the President's brother...

"In our negotiations with the Americans during the crisis, they had, on the whole, been open and candid with us, especially Robert Kennedy."

NIKITA KHRUSHCHEV

"... I call upon Chairman Khrushchev to halt and eliminate this clandestine, reckless, and provocative threat to world peace and to stable relations between our two nations. I call upon him further to abandon this course of world domination, and to join in an historic effort to end the perilous arms race and to transform the history of man ...

"We have no wish to war with the Soviet Union — for we are a peaceful people who desire to live in peace with all other peoples ...

"The path we have chosen for the present is full of hazards, as all paths are — but it is the one most consistent with our character and courage as a nation. The cost of freedom is always high — but Americans have always paid it. And one path we shall never choose, and that is the path of surrender or submission.

"Our goal is not the victory of might, but the vindication of right — not peace at the expense of freedom, but both peace and freedom ..."

JOHN F. KENNEDY
From a radio and television broadcast, October 22, 1962

"... As I read your letter October 26th, the key elements of your proposals are as follows:

"1. You would agree to remove these weapons systems from Cuba under appropriate United Nations observation and supervision; and undertake, with suitable safeguards, to halt the further introduction of such weapons systems into Cuba.

"2. We, on our part, would agree — upon the establishment of adequate arrangements through the United Nations to ensure the carrying out and continuation of these commitments — (a) to remove promptly the quarantine measures now in effect and (b) to give assurances against an invasion of Cuba ...

"I would like to say again that the United States is very much interested in reducing tensions and halting the arms race; and if your letter signifies that you are prepared to discuss a detente affecting NATO and the Warsaw Pact, we are quite prepared to consider with our allies any useful proposals."

JOHN F. KENNEDY
Letter to Chairman Khrushchev, October 26, 1962

The men who had been directly responsible for "nuclear disarmament" negotiations: Dean Rusk, the Secretary of State, John J. McCloy and Arthur Dean (left to right). Now all hope was vanishing.

From left, McGeorge Bundy, National Security Adviser to the President, the President, General Maxwell Taylor and Defense Secretary Robert McNamara, conferring at the White House portico during the crisis.

"The dominant feeling at the meeting was stunned surprise. No one had expected or anticipated that the Russians would deploy surface-to-surface ballistic missiles in Cuba . . .

"I told Ambassador Dobrynin of President Kennedy's deep concern about what was happening. He told me I should not be concerned, for he was instructed by Soviet Chairman Nikita S. Khrushchev to assure President Kennedy that there would be no . . . offensive weapons placed in Cuba . . . I could assure the President that Khrushchev would do nothing to disrupt the relationship of our two countries, he liked President Kennedy and did not wish to embarrass him . . .

"Now, as the representatives of the CIA explained the U-2 photographs that morning, Tuesday, October 16, we realized that it had all been lies, one gigantic fabric of lies. The Russians were putting missiles in Cuba . . .

"Neither side wanted war over Cuba, but it was possible that either side could take steps that for reasons of 'security' or 'pride' or 'face' — would require a response by the other side, which, in turn, would bring about a counter-response and eventually an escalation into armed conflict. That was what he wanted to avoid . . . We were not going to misjudge, or miscalculate, or challenge the other side needlessly, or push our adversaries into a course of action that was not intended or anticipated.

"I think these few minutes were the time of gravest concern for the President. Was the world on the brink of a holocaust? Was it our error? A mistake? Was there something further that should have been done? Or not done? His hand went up to his face and covered his mouth. He opened and closed his fist. His face seemed drawn, his eyes pained, almost gray. We stared at each other across the table. For a few fleeting seconds, it was almost as though no one else was there and he was no longer the President.

"Inexplicably, I thought of when he was ill and almost died; when he lost his child; when we learned that our oldest brother had been killed; of personal times of strain and hurt . . . 'Isn't there some way we can avoid having our first exchange with a Russian submarine?' 'No . . . There is no alternative,' said McNamara.

"The minutes in the Cabinet Room ticked slowly by . . . then it was 10:25 — a messenger brought in a note to John McCone. 'Mr. President, we have a preliminary report which seems to indicate that some of the Russian ships have stopped dead in the water.' "

ROBERT F. KENNEDY

"For a moment the world had stood still, and now it was going around again . . ."
ROBERT F. KENNEDY

"I could not accept the idea that the United States would rain bombs on Cuba . . . whatever validity the military and political arguments were for an attack . . . America's traditions and history would not permit such a course of action. They were in the last analysis, advocating a surprise attack by a very large nation against a very small one . . . Our struggle against Communism throughout the world was far more than physical survival — it had as its essence our heritage and our ideals, and these we must not destroy."

ROBERT F. KENNEDY

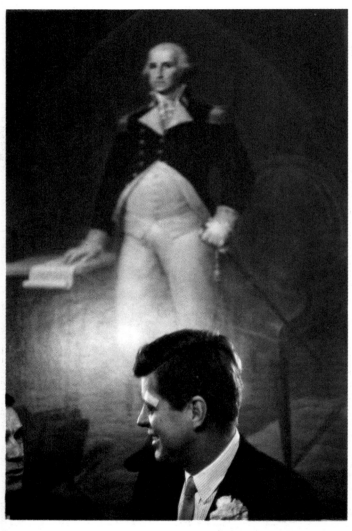

President Kennedy hosts a party for Congressmen.
St. Patrick's Day, 1961.

Ex-President Harry Truman seemed to propel President Kennedy's sense of humour to ever greater heights. At the Alfred E. Smith Memorial Dinner in October of 1960, which featured both candidate Nixon and candidate Kennedy, he responded to ex-President Truman's earlier statement that those who voted Republican could go to "hell", by saying:

"... Mr. Nixon, like the rest of us, has had his troubles in this campaign. At one point even the Wall Street Journal was criticizing his tactics. That is like the Osservatore Romano criticizing the Pope.

"One of the inspiring notes that was struck in the last debate was struck by the Vice President in his very moving warning to the candidates against the use of profanity by presidents and ex-presidents when they are on the stump. And I know after fourteen years in the Congress with the Vice President, that he was very sincere in his views about the use of profanity. But I am told that a prominent Republican said to him yesterday in Jacksonville, Florida, 'Mr. Vice President, that was a damn fine speech.' And the Vice President said, 'I appreciate the compliment but not the language.' And the Republican went on, 'Yes, sir, I liked it so much that I contributed a thousand dollars to your campaign.' And Mr. Nixon replied, 'The hell you say.'

"However, I would not want to give the impression that I am taking former President Truman's use of language lightly. I have sent him the following wire:

" 'Dear Mr. President: I have noted with interest your suggestion as to where those who vote for my opponent should go. While I understand and sympathize with your deep motivation, I think it is important that our side try to refrain from raising the religious issue.' "

When the ex-President returned to the White House as the guest of the Kennedys in November 1961 and entertained the assembled guests by playing the piano, the President remarked:

"Don't say there is no justice in the world, Stalin has been kicked out of Lenin's tomb and President Truman is back in the White House."

Ex-President Truman at the White House piano.

Left: Caroline and John-John continued to delight an indulgent President, watching their antics from the Oval Office. Caroline's favourite pony, Macaroni, at one time had invaded the historic chamber. This time he was stopped at the very door to the presidential office.

"Caroline, have you been eating candy?"
No answer.
"Caroline," the President repeated, *"have you been eating candy? Answer yes, no or maybe."*

March on Washington

"Nineteen sixty-three is not an end, but a beginning. And those who hope that the Negro needed to blow off steam and will now be content, will have a rude awakening if the nation returns to business as usual. There will be neither rest nor tranquillity in America until the Negro is granted his citizenship rights. The whirlwinds of the revolt will continue to shake the foundations of our nation until the bright day of justice emerges.

"Let us not seek to satisfy our thirst for freedom by drinking from the cup of bitterness and hatred. We must forever conduct our struggle on the high plane of dignity and discipline. We must not allow our creative protest to generate into physical violence. Again and again we must rise to the majestic heights of meeting physical force with soul force; and the marvelous new militancy, which has engulfed the Negro community, must not lead us to a distrust of all white people. For many of our white brothers, as evidenced by their presence here today, have come to realize that their destiny is tied up with our destiny. And they have come to realize that their freedom is inextricably bound to our freedom. We cannot walk alone.

"I have a dream that one day this nation will rise up and live out the true meaning of its creed, 'We hold these truths to be self-evident, that all men are created equal.' I have a dream that one day on the red hills of Georgia, sons of former slaves and the sons of former slave owners will be able to sit down together at the table of brotherhood.

"I have a dream today!

"I have a dream that one day down in Alabama — with its vicious racists, with its Governor having his lips dripping with the words of interposition and nullification — one day right there in Alabama, little black boys and black girls will be able to join hands with little white boys and white girls as sisters and brothers.

"I have a dream today!

"I have a dream that one day 'every valley shall be exalted and every hill and mountain shall be made low. The rough places will be made plain and the crooked places will be made straight, and the glory of the Lord shall be revealed, and all flesh shall see it together.'

"This is our hope. This is the faith that I go back to the South with. With the faith we shall be able to transform the jangling discords of our nation into a beautiful symphony of brotherhood. With this faith we will be able to work together, to pray together, to struggle together, to go to jail together, to stand up for freedom together, knowing that we will be free one day. And this will be the day. This will be the day when all of God's children will be able to sing with new meaning, 'My country 'tis of thee, sweet land of liberty, of thee I sing. Land where my fathers died, land of the pilgrim's pride, from every mountain side, let freedom ring.' And if America is to be a great nation, this must become true.

"So let freedom ring from the prodigious hilltops of New Hampshire; let freedom ring from the mighty mountains of New York; let freedom ring from the heightening Alleghenies of Pennsylvania; let freedom ring from the snow-capped Rockies of Colorado; let freedom ring from the curvaceous slopes of California. But not only that. Let freedom ring from Stone Mountain of Georgia; let freedom ring from Lookout Mountain of Tennessee; let freedom ring from every hill and molehill of Mississippi. From every mountainside, let freedom ring.

"And when this happens, and when we allow freedom to ring, when we let it ring from every village and every hamlet, from every state and every city, we will be able to speed up that day when all God's children, black men and white men, Jews and gentiles, Protestants and Catholics, will be able to join hands and sing in the words of the old Negro spiritual: 'Free at last. Free at last. Thank God Almighty, we are free at last.' "

MARTIN LUTHER KING JR.
from "I Have A Dream", August 28, 1963

Martin Luther King Jr. at the Lincoln Memorial in Washington DC, delivering his "I Have A Dream" speech before an audience estimated to number nearly 500,000, the largest demonstration in the history of the civil rights struggle.

THE KENNEDY STYLE GOES ABROAD

Paris · Vienna · London · Berlin · Ireland · Mexico

Jacqueline Kennedy at the Elysée Palace reception.

"I do not think it altogether inappropriate to introduce myself to this audience. I am the man who accompanied Jacqueline Kennedy to Paris, and I have enjoyed it."

JOHN F. KENNEDY
Press Luncheon, Paris, June 2, 1961

President Kennedy arriving at the Palais de Chaillot.

"You must remember that I wasn't recalled to office as my country's saviour."

JOHN F. KENNEDY, to a reporter who had asked what he thought about de Gaulle's imperious handling of French press photographers

"... if we value so highly the presence in Paris of a President of the United States, it is also because that President is yourself. Let me tell you how greatly Frenchmen have admired your intelligence and courage since you first grasped, in your turn and in today's heavy seas, the helm of the American ship of state. Already we have discerned in you the philosophy of the true statesman, who chooses his goal, who holds his course, who is neither halted nor diverted by vicissitudes, and who looks to no easy formula or expedient to lighten the responsibility which is his burden and his honour."

CHARLES DE GAULLE, in a toast to President Kennedy at the Formal Dinner in the Elysée Palace, May 31, 1961
The two men would spend nearly eight hours, spread over three days, in intimate conversation. They parted with great mutual esteem.

The reception at the Elysée in honour of President and Mrs. Kennedy was the highlight of the season. The cream of society attended the reception and the President, in tails, and his wife, wearing a stunning gown, were lionized. President de Gaulle, in dress uniform and wearing his medals, took the young President around; he seemed to enjoy himself immensely. For us, the photographers (three in all), it had been a trying day. Our instructions had called for black tie, but on the afternoon of the event they had been changed to white tie. The stores were closed. Moreover the rule was not to mix with the guests, but to stay on a special platform, guarded by alert and elaborately dressed security police, far from the action. We escaped, leaving behind the guards, who were not allowed to mingle either and stood, furious, behind red velvet ropes. When President Kennedy, aware of the rule, spotted me, he leaned over with a twinkle in his eye and whispered in my ear, "If they cut your balls off, Jacques, for mixing with the better classes, do not expect the President of the United States to come to your aid."

Jacqueline Kennedy with Madame de Gaulle to her right.

Rose Kennedy at the reception.

Vienna

"I had met Kennedy in Vienna. He impressed me as a better statesman than Eisenhower. Unlike Eisenhower, Kennedy had a precisely formulated opinion on every subject. I joked with him that we had cast the deciding ballot in his election to the presidency over that son-of-a-bitch Richard Nixon. When he asked me what I meant, I explained that by waiting to release the U-2 pilot Gary Powers until after the American election, we kept Nixon from being able to claim that he could deal with the Russians . . ."

NIKITA KHRUSHCHEV

Actually, according to Pierre Salinger, who interviewed Khrushchev at length, the Chairman was confusing pilots. He meant the R B 47 pilot and not the U-2 pilot.

> ## "It's going to be a cold winter."
> JOHN F. KENNEDY's parting statement to Chairman Khrushchev

A great part of President Kennedy's conversations with Charles de Gaulle had concerned Chairman Khrushchev, whom he was now meeting for the first time, and whom he was eager to size up and understand. De Gaulle had stated that Khrushchev would threaten to seize West Berlin and to sign a separate treaty with East Germany within six months. He had considered the Russian Premier a bluffer and warned Kennedy to pay no attention. "He's been saying that for three years. When the six months are up, he postpones the treaty with East Germany for another six months, and then another six months. He'll never sign that treaty because Russia does not want a war." So now Kennedy, who had been well briefed on his adversary's personality and had read everything about him, stood back and took a good look.

The meetings switched back and forth between the American and the Russian embassies and they changed from furious confrontations on the part of Khrushchev to light banter. Dave Powers and Kenny O'Donnell in the book *Johnny, We Hardly Knew Ye*, give a succinct and amusing account of the events. The President, with his back acting up again, spent a great deal of his time soaking in a tub, where he would recall the day's events. Over lunch the President asked what medal the Chairman was wearing. "The Lenin peace medal," was the answer. Said the President laconically, "I hope you get to keep it." But the Berlin threat was indeed raised precisely as de Gaulle had predicted, with such vehemence that Kennedy was shaken. At their last private meeting Khrushchev flatly threatened Kennedy with war if the United States insisted on defending its rights in West Berlin after Russia signed a separate treaty with East Germany, to which Kennedy replied: "It's going to be a cold winter."

> ## "I considered the Vienna talks to be useful. The somber mood that they conveyed was not cause for elation or relaxation, nor was it cause for undue pessimism or fear."
> JOHN F. KENNEDY
> Report to the American People, June 6, 1961

At the reception given by the Austrian President for Kennedy and Khrushchev and their staffs at Schoenbrunn Palace, the Russian Chairman sat next to Jacqueline Kennedy, openly admiring her and keeping up a constant stream of jokes. The President had a more difficult time, for Mrs. Khrushchev was reserved and hardly spoke all night.

London

From Vienna, we flew directly to London, where the President was to be godfather to his sister-in-law Lee Radziwill's baby and where he was to confer with Prime Minister Macmillan on his recent meetings with President de Gaulle and Chairman Khrushchev. It was a private visit, and the President stayed at the Radziwill house in Buckingham Place. He addressed the staff at the US embassy, conferred with Macmillan for roughly four hours and he and Mrs. Kennedy had dinner with the Queen and Prince Philip. In forty-eight hours we were on our way home. But for me the visit had its problems. Because it was a private visit, there were to be no interviews, no photographs, and the christening ceremony was totally closed to the press.

President Kennedy during the christening ceremony of Anna Christina Radziwill, his niece, at Westminster Cathedral. *Left:* Signing the register.

Still, some 2000 reporters were covering the trip and were clamouring for news. I was escorted by both the Secret Service and Scotland Yard to Westminster Cathedral, where the ceremony was to take place in a crypt. Nuns lined the long underground passage and the President stopped to chat with them. Afterwards, a reception was being held at the Radziwills' house and some local residents were startled as Scotland Yard detectives, one man wearing a bowler hat, took me through back gardens and over roofs to reach the party. I had wanted a few of my photographs to be released to the general press, but Mrs. Kennedy vetoed the idea and to this day I stand accused of having made a deal with a major publication and refusing to hand out the photographs. I wish to set the record straight; I didn't.

President and Mrs. Kennedy at the Radziwill party.

Lee Radziwill welcomes Douglas Fairbanks Jr.

The party at 4 Buckingham Place was a joyous affair and lasted for hours. It was as though, being back in a friendly and English-speaking country, the nightmare of a threatened war over Berlin, the disagreements over Laos and the general bullying Khrushchev had engaged in, had never happened. The President had stayed remarkably calm throughout his trying meetings and now he was relaxed, the only official business being his conferences with Macmillan. No one talked of the days just passed. No one discussed what was, after all, the President's first public exposure abroad, wide open to judgment by the world's press.

Jacqueline Kennedy in animated conversation.

The meetings in London were an exchange between friends who basically agreed with each other. But the meeting in Vienna was to bear results as well. Khrushchev's first gesture after Vienna was to send Kennedy two gifts, the model of an American whaler and a puppy, "Pushkina", offspring of the famous Sputnik dog that travelled in outer space, together with a conciliatory letter. Instead of going to war in Berlin he built a wall, which Kennedy said was the lesser of two evils. And four months later the Russians began to talk. Another offer was made on Berlin, which Kennedy turned down. After the death of Dag Hammarskjöld, the United Nations Secretary General, the Russians had insisted that he be replaced by a troika, rather than one Secretary General. President Kennedy had denounced this move, and when the Russian Foreign Minister came to see him he was prepared for Gromyko in his own very special way. With a smile Kennedy handed him two leather-bound volumes of Russian fables by Ivan Andreevich Krylov, the Russian Aesop, and opened one at his favourite. Gromyko read it, laughed, and somehow the ice was broken; communications had been re-established. Ten days later Khrushchev announced the withdrawal of the troika proposal and soon thereafter he dropped his threat of a treaty with East Germany.

Prime Minister Harold Macmillan at the party.

When partners with each other don't
  agree
Each project must a failure be,
And out of it, no profit come but sheer
  vexation.
A Swan, a Pike and Crab once took
  their station
In harness, and would drag a loaded
  cart;
But when the moment came for
  them to start,
They sweat, they strain, and yet the
  cart stands still;
What's lacking?
The load must, as it seemed, have
  been but light;
The Swan, though, to the clouds
  takes flight,
The Pike into the water pulls, the Crab
  keeps backing.
Now which of them was right, which
  wrong, concerns us not;
The cart is still upon the selfsame
  spot.

  IVAN ANDREEVICH KRYLOV
  A Fable

President Kennedy and Pierre Salinger. The issue was the headlines describing the previous day's meeting with Khrushchev as a defeat for the American President. The President felt that he had come out well, that the meeting had produced worthwhile results and that the press was being unfair.

Mexico

Jacqueline Kennedy at the airport ceremonies in Mexico City, June 29, 1962.

The tumultuous reception of the President's motolcade.

"I believe that there is so much which unites this great country with my own. We share a border of 2000 miles. Over 3 million of our citizens in the United States are descended from your citizens. Most of all, we are both children of revolution, and it is my hope that the spirit of our revolution in the United States is as alive today in our country as is the spirit of your revolution here in Mexico. That revolution in our country and, in a sense, in yours, was primarily political, a declaration of political liberty . . ."

JOHN F. KENNEDY
On arrival in Mexico City, June 29, 1962

"We in the United States are committed to a better life for our people, for no nation can seek social justice abroad that does not practice it at home. But now, in addition, the United States of America is committed to help fulfill these goals throughout the Americas, to work together with Mexico and all the other nations of the inter-American system, to create a society in which all men have equal access to land, to jobs, and to education — a society in which no man is exploited for the enrichment of a few, and in which every arm of the government is dedicated to the welfare of all the people . . .

"We are devoted to the increasing social justice of all. National independence, the fact of political freedom, means very little to the man who is not yet independent of poverty and illiteracy and disease. New factories and machinery mean little to the family without a home, to the student without a meal, to the farmer who gives up hope of finally owning the land that he tills . . .

"It will not be easy . . . Ending the outmoded systems of land tenure, reforming unjust systems of taxation, expanding the opportunities for better housing and better health and better education . . . all this will not be easy . . ."

JOHN F. KENNEDY
From an address at a luncheon given in his honour by
President López Mateos, June 29, 1962

Berlin

The President with Mayor Willy Brandt, later to become the Chancellor of Germany, and Chancellor Konrad Adenauer (right), the towering post-war figure who took a country in ruins and bewilderment and steered it towards a new and vital democracy.

"There are many people in the world who really don't understand, or say they don't, what is the great issue between the free world and the Communist world. Let them come to Berlin. There are some who say that Communism is the wave of the future. Let them come to Berlin. And there are some who say in Europe and elsewhere we can work with the Communists. Let them come to Berlin. And there are even a few who say that it is true that Communism is an evil system, but it permits us to make economic progress. 'Lass sie nach Berlin kommen.' Let them come to Berlin.

"Freedom has many difficulties and democracy is not perfect, but we have never had to put a wall up to keep our people in, to prevent them from leaving us…

"I know of no town, no city, that has been besieged for eighteen years that still lives with the vitality and the force, and the hope and the determination of the city of West Berlin. While the wall is the most obvious and vivid demonstration of the failures of the Communist system, for all the world to see, we take no satisfaction in it, for it is … an offense not only against history but an offense against humanity, separating families, dividing husbands and wives and brothers and sisters, and dividing a people who wish to be joined together.

"What is true of this city is true of Germany — real, lasting peace in Europe can never be assured as long as one German out of four is denied the elementary right of free men, and that is to make a free choice.

"Freedom is indivisible, and when one man is enslaved, all are not free…

"All free men, wherever they may live, are citizens of Berlin, and therefore, as a free man, I take pride in the words 'Ich bin ein Berliner…' "

JOHN F. KENNEDY
Rudolf Wilde Platz, June 26, 1963

The President speaking to his largest-ever audience outside the United States at the Rudolph Wilde Platz in West Berlin on June 26, 1963. The President's words *"Ich bin ein Berliner"* (I am a Berliner) caused near riots of joy and emotion.

"Prince Bismarck once said that one-third of the students of German universities broke down from overwork; another third broke down from dissipation, and the other third ruled Germany. I do not know which third of the student body is here today, but I am confident that I am talking to the future rulers of this country…

"In the fifteen turbulent years since this institution was founded, dedicated to the motto 'Truth, Justice, and Liberty', much has changed… West Berlin has been blockaded, threatened, harassed, but it continues to grow in industry and culture and size, and in the hearts of free men. Germany has changed. Western Europe and, indeed, the entire world have changed, but this university has maintained its fidelity to these three ideals…

"The cause of human rights and dignity, some two centuries after its birth, in Europe and the United States, is still moving men and nations with ever-increasing momentum. The Negro citizens of my own country have strengthened their demand for equality and opportunity. And the American people and the American government are going to respond. The pace of decolonization has quickened in Africa. The people of the developing nations have intensified their pursuit of economic and social justice. The people of Eastern Europe, even after eighteen years of oppression, are not immune to change. The truth doesn't die. The desire for liberty cannot be fully suppressed…

"When the possibilities of reconciliation appear, we in the West will make it clear that we are not hostile to any people or system providing they choose their own destiny without interfering with the free choice of others. There will be wounds to heal and suspicions to be eased on both sides. Fair and effective agreements to end the arms race must be reached. These changes will not come today or tomorrow. But our efforts for a real settlement must continue undiminished."

JOHN F. KENNEDY
The Free University of Berlin, June 26, 1963

Ireland

President Kennedy being greeted by his cousin Mary Kennedy Ryan of County Wexford. Looking on, his sisters Jean Smith and Eunice Shriver.

*"Cousin Jack came here like an ordinary member of the family. He crouched at the fire
and blew the bellows. He asked . . . about the family and the farm . . . He said,
'The fire feels wonderful.' Oh, he cared — he really gave you the feeling he cared . . .
"Cousins came from miles around. He shook hands with each of them, and he said, 'I'm
glad some of the Kennedys missed the boat and didn't all go to Washington.' We had tea
from a silver pot and cold boiled salmon . . . The sisters were lovely too. Not a bit of false
pride in them, for all their money. They sprang up and down to help with the servin' . . .
"The government men with him kept telling him he had to go — that he must be on
schedule . . . His last words were, 'Cousin Mary, the next time I come I'll bring Jackie and
the children' . . . Do you know that angel woman wrote back and thanked me for being
so kind to her Jack?"*

MARY KENNEDY RYAN

"When my great grandfather left here to become a cooper in East Boston, he carried nothing with him except two things: a strong religious faith and a strong desire for liberty. I am glad to say that all of his great grandchildren have valued that inheritance . . ."

JOHN F. KENNEDY, New Ross, June 27, 1963

"This is not the land of my birth, but it is the land for which I hold the greatest affection, and I certainly will come back in the springtime . . ."

JOHN F. KENNEDY, Limerick, June 29, 1963

"We went into this little room, with a fireplace, to see Mrs. Ryan. I was carrying the gifts Jack was giving them. He didn't realize he had that many cousins — there were more than we had presents for. Cousin Jimmy hands him a shot of Irish whiskey — it looked to me like a glass. He slipped it over to me and said to get rid of that — which meant to drink it — I downed it and 'Oh my God,' in the helicopter he said, 'imagine drinking so early in the morning' . . . There was nothing like the days in Ireland."

DAVID F. POWERS

" 'Tis it is the Shannon's brightly glancing stream,
Brightly gleaming, silent in the morning beam,
Oh, the sight entrancing,
Thus returns from travels long,
Years of exile, years of pain,
To see old Shannon's face again,
O'er the waters dancing."

JOHN F. KENNEDY quoting "On the River Shannon" by
Gerald Griffin, on leaving Ireland

"The 13th day of December, 1882, will be a day long remembered in American history. At Fredericksburg, Va., thousands of men fought and died on one of the bloodiest battlefields of the American Civil War. One of the most brilliant stories of that day was written by a band of 1200 men who went into battle wearing a green sprig in their hats. They bore a proud heritage and a special courage, given to those who had long fought for the cause of freedom. I am referring, of course, to the Irish Brigade. General Robert E. Lee, the great military leader of the Southern Confederate forces, said of this group of men after the battle, 'The gallant stand which this bold brigade made on the heights of Fredericksburg is well known. Never were men so brave. They ennobled their race by their splendid gallantry on that desperate occasion. Their brilliant though hopeless assaults on our lines excited the hearty applause of our officers and soldiers.'

"Of the 1200 men who took part in that assault, 280 survived the battle. The Irish Brigade was led into battle on that occasion by Brig. Gen. Thomas F. Meagher, who had participated in the unsuccessful Irish uprising of 1848, was captured by the British and sent in a prison ship to Australia, from whence he finally came to America. In the fall of 1862, after serving with distinction and gallantry in some of the toughest fighting of this most bloody struggle, the Irish Brigade was presented with a new set of flags. In the city ceremony, the city chamberlain gave them the motto, 'The Union, our Country, and Ireland Forever.' Their old ones having been torn to shreds by bullets in previous battles, Capt. Richard McGee took possession of these flags on December 2nd in New York City and arrived with them at the Battle of Fredericksburg and carried them in the battle. Today, in recognition of what these gallant Irishmen and what millions of other Irish have done for my country, and through the generosity of the 'Fighting 69th', I would like to present one of these flags to the people of Ireland...

"I am deeply honored to be your guest in the Free Parliament of a free Ireland. If this nation had achieved its present political and economic stature a century or so ago, my great grandfather might never have left New Ross, and I might, if fortunate, be sitting down there with you. Of course, if your own President had never left Brooklyn, he might be standing up here instead of me...!"

JOHN F. KENNEDY
Dublin, June 28, 1963

CHARMED LIVES

A Family Album

Grandpa Kennedy and Caroline in Hyannis Port, 1958.

"*He wasn't around as much as some fathers; but . . . he made his children feel that they were the most important things in the world to him.*"
JOHN F. KENNEDY talking about his father

Jacqueline, Caroline and John F. Kennedy at their house in Hyannis Port.

"Jack has never done a good job at relaxing, but Jackie has gone a long way to change that."
EUNICE SHRIVER

On the *Marlin,* the family cruiser, off Hyannis Port. From left Pat, Jean and Ethel Kennedy with children.

Much has been written about the closeness of the family, the softball games, the lively dinner conversation, the encouragement all gave each other, and summers were the best time to observe the pleasure they derived from each other's company. The Kennedy compound, as it became known, consists of three houses with one lawn rolling down to the dunes and the sea between them: the "big" house belonging to the father, where the children grew up and which was now used for an overflow of guests and friends, Robert's house and John Kennedy's house, the smallest. The houses, typically New England white clapboard structures, were simply and comfortably furnished in bright colours and simple rugs, ready to receive dozens of little feet, still covered with sand or dew.

There would be a constant stream of people going back and forth between the houses, children would eat wherever they happened to be at mealtimes, and different groups of adults and children would engage in different activities in different places. And then there was the sea. John F. Kennedy loved the sea. He was a superb sailor, going out often, even in murky weather. And he loved to swim and tumble in the water with his children, and nieces and nephews.

A clutch of Kennedys and friends at Hickory Hill.

"He'd rather, I'm sure, have walked the beach with Caroline at the Cape than have met Khrushchev in Vienna."
TORBERT MACDONALD

"Do you remember the night that Patrick died? The Secret Service awakened me. The baby was dying and no one wanted to tell him. I had to. It's about four in the morning. We're on a ward and this baby, in some sort of a chamber has been burned. He looks in — and nothing looks worse than a child that's been burned. I guess the bed caught on fire and the burns were on the chest. He said, 'Dave, call the nurse.' She was avoiding him because she knew the news was bad. She's telling him what happened to the baby, she tells him the mother comes and visits — the baby can't feel a thing, looks awful. He said 'What's the mother's name?', and he wrote to the lady and said, 'Keep up your courage,' signed John F. Kennedy. Now here's a man who's going down and having his own child die and still had time for someone else. He had such great compassion for people."

DAVID F. POWERS

Eunice Shriver with retarded children in a pony cart; and, right above, with the President; and, right below, during a ball game.

Ever since it became clear that one of John Kennedy's sisters, Rosemary, suffered from a form of mental retardation, the family has been deeply involved in helping the retarded. The Joseph P. Kennedy Jr. Foundation, formed for the purpose, finances schools for the retarded, helps hospitals and special clinics to deal with the retarded and finances specialist research into the disease. Each year, Eunice Kennedy Shriver gives a party for retarded children at her home, which includes games, pony rides, ice cream and other delights and in which her own and other Kennedy children participate. The President, throughout his life, concerned himself deeply with the problem. His personal experience perhaps explains his impassioned fights for better and more hospital care and nursing services as well as his and Robert's compassion for those in need.

Hickory Hill had been the headquarters of General George B. McClellan during the Civil War. It was a spacious manor house surrounded by more than five acres of rolling countryside and lawn. By 1957 there were stables, a swimming pool and tennis courts on the property. Here Ethel Kennedy helps her oldest daughter Kathleen with the pony, while a friend waits. On the right, Bobby runs with David.

"The first time I remember meeting Bobby was when he was three-and-a-half, one summer on the Cape."

JOHN F. KENNEDY

Bobby and children at Hyannis Port, followed by Meegan, one of his two lumbering, oversized and sometimes bad-tempered dogs.

Oh, it was a glorious experience, entering the Robert Kennedy home for the first time. I remember the first night coming to dinner, having spent the day with Robert on Capitol Hill. They had five children then and they had recently bought Hickory Hill, their house in McLean, Virginia, from the John Kennedys, for whom the place had become too big and empty after Jacqueline's miscarriage. I had known Robert for some time in my role as a magazine photographer covering the up-and-coming investigator. He had been sober and serious, revealing sudden flashes of humour, and sometimes anger; but I was not prepared for the man I met on coming to the house late that night. All of his reserve seemed to melt in the glory of his family, and the long, difficult day was forgotten in the warmth of love of a father for his children and vice versa. It was chaos, with all the children talking at once and Bobby answering each of them with humour and sometimes trying to be stern, at which he didn't fully succeed. Ethel instantly accepted this stranger into their house, and later on I had to go upstairs to say the evening prayers with the children, which took place after a family pillow fight.

Mary Kerry and Courtney with rabbit.   Michael with geese.

The planning for the annual Christmas card, which always seemed to feature one more child, was not a task to be taken lightly. Around July Ethel would become nervous that no theme had been worked out, and frantic telephone calls and conferences would ensue, to which all within earshot would contribute. By the great day everything would have been worked out in a precise fashion. The theme, what the children would wear, the shape of the card, the design of the card were all debated with great enthusiasm. The children themselves, having to give up their games, send home their friends and pose "once more" for hours on end, were less enthusiastic than their elders. I remember one year when the children, wearing white nightgowns, carried lighted candles. Another year the theme was to be the animals from the grounds. I remember three hysterical adults, including Ethel, shooing geese all over the place, with Michael going in one direction and the geese in the other, to the despair of all present. The card was finally produced and declared a major success. There were seven children that year. I believe the Christmas in question was 1961, the first year of the New Frontier.

"For a while at Hickory Hill, they had one of those dwarf ponies, about as big as a dog. Then they had a seal who lived in the swimming pool. He was named Sandy. One day, he got out of the pool and started down the road towards McLean. Now he lives at the zoo. They also had a honey bear — a nocturnal animal that was always climbing around at night, and getting into the icebox. In the daytime, he'd be sleeping in the bookcases, doing heaven knows what damage . . .
"The coati-mundi . . . a frightening animal, some relation to an anteater . . . actually bit Ethel."
KAY EVANS, a family friend

David with goats.

Bobby Jr. with Meegan and Brumus.

The Attorney General with his four sons.

Evenings at Hickory Hill. Kathleen on a donkey pulled by her father.

Kathleen dressed as a fairy with David.

"I was in charge of finding movies for them to show out there at Hickory Hill . . . You had to please the audience from four to eighty . . . It was quite difficult . . . The movie would come on, and a well-developed girl would walk across the screen, and everybody would look at the children and then they'd look at me and say 'George!' Then the children would all be sent off to bed . . . I was the villain to young and old alike."

GEORGE STEVENS, Director, American Film Institute

"I don't want my young children to be brought up by nurses and Secret Service men."
JACQUELINE KENNEDY

"He loved his children. I was so happy when Jack finally got in the White House. He spent so much time with them. Every night, no matter what's going on, he'd say I want them brought over before they go to bed. He had breakfast with them and lunch with them. There's something going on, like the Cuban missile crisis, he'd go up to look at that boy. One day, the President's with some ambassador, Caroline's on Macaroni and he goes and yells 'Caroline', and she rode the thing right through the rose garden right into the White House office. He didn't care. He loved it.

"And Jackie was great. The day of the funeral was John's third birthday. We came back to the White House and went-upstairs. It was Teddy, Bobby and myself and Jackie, Lee and the children. And she was singing Happy Birthday to John — everybody had a lump in their throat. Gives you a chill."

DAVID F. POWERS

Nurse Maud Shaw with Caroline and Michael and Stevie Smith.

Maria Shriver.

Stevie Smith, Caroline and Michael.

John with Nurse Shaw and William K. Smith.

Eunice Shriver and her daughter Maria.

Summer picnics were the favourite outings of young and old alike during these wonderful Cape Cod days. Basket upon basket would be filled with hot dogs and hard-boiled eggs, hamburgers and marshmallows, cokes and beer. All the Kennedy children and their friends and pets would crowd into the *Marlin,* and motor over to some nearby island such as Great Island or Cotuit. There on the beach a barbecue would be set up, baseball bats and footballs would come out and the children and the grown-ups would partake in the simple joy of living. Sometimes the throng would be thirty or more and several boats were needed. Oh, what fun it was, what joy.

Bobby Kennedy, holding David's hand, talking to Eunice and Senator Kennedy at Teddy Kennedy's wedding.

Rose and Senator Kennedy at Teddy Kennedy's wedding.

Joan, Mrs. Edward Kennedy, with her daughter Kara at their house in Boston's Beacon Hill section.

The living room at John Kennedy's house in Hyannis Port.

Life outside the immediate family could become lonely. "The presidency is no place to make new friends," Kennedy had said and Jacqueline tried hard to bring up her children as normally as possible, explaining that the White House was only a temporary residence.

"In eleven weeks I went from Senator to President, and in that short space of time I inherited Laos, Cuba, Berlin, the nuclear threat and all the rest. It was a terrific adjustment to make. I've made it now, but naturally there have been some changes. It's certainly true that I'm more isolated socially. In the beginning I tried to carry on the life I had led, going out, seeing people; but I soon realized that was impossible. Apart from state dinners I suppose I see only three or four people socially. But I have no feeling of withdrawing. After all, everyone's life is circumscribed . . ."

JOHN F. KENNEDY

Caroline Kennedy in Hyannis Port.

"It was six years of our marriage, anyway, of every single moment of free time going out — and that was the way it was gotten."

JACQUELINE KENNEDY explaining how her husband got the nomination

"I cast only one vote — for Jack. It is a rare thing to be able to vote for one's husband for President of the United States, and I didn't want to dilute it by voting for anyone else."

JACQUELINE KENNEDY

"He loved children and told Jacqueline before their marriage that he wanted at least five; she had four in seven years. He liked young children in particular and always wanted a baby coming along when its predecessor was growing up."

ARTHUR SCHLESINGER Jr.

Ethel Kennedy at Hickory Hill, reading to her children (from left) Bobby, Joe, Mary Kerry, Kathleen and Michael. Standing up are David and Mary Courtney. The painting in the background is of Bobby and David.

"I asked my children and they voted 'yes' by four to three with two abstentions."
ROBERT KENNEDY in response to a seven-year-old asking whether he treated his children well

Jackie painting in Hyannis Port with Caroline.
Right: With her sister Lee Radziwill and children.

"*Making the learning process part game, part work, brings excitement to the child, and eagerness to do well . . . The praise that comes from a parent encourages the child more.*"
JACQUELINE KENNEDY

Ethel Kennedy in pursuit of her husband during a football game at Hickory Hill.

Competition was fierce in whatever contest was in progress, whether a softball game or some more intellectual pursuit. It was fiercest when the Kennedys played against the non-Kennedys, or the not yet Kennedys, as Jackie, who was not a natural born football player, would relate later about her time as Senator Kennedy's fiancée. (She broke her ankle and retired from the sport.) But fierce competition in all areas of life was part of Bobby's make-up, instilled by the father, and taken to heart by the son. He competed not only against other human beings, but against nature itself. Displaying great physical courage he shot the rapids of Idaho's 'River of No Return' in a kayak, scaled Canada's Mount Kennedy, and was a daring skier, and, while others jested about the President's fifty-mile-hike-fitness-programme, he was the only known member of the administration who actually completed that task. To those who went with him and failed he said: "You're lucky your brother isn't the President."

"He was an accomplished skier — with a style that was rugged and challenging . . . He liked to keep just on the edge of control . . . It was the same on Mount Kennedy . . . He had no training in mountains. He was afraid of heights and he'd shake. And yet on that climb, I had continually to pick up the pace . . . At the top . . . I stopped and belayed him up to me. The crest was about fifty feet away. We trailed him as he broke through . . . to the summit. It was pretty emotional — to reach the top of the mountain honoring his brother. He was very concerned to get there."

JIM WHITTAKER, mountaineer and family friend

Grandfather and father beam down upon David Kennedy posing for the camera with Meegan at his side, Hyannis Port.

THE SHOTS IN DALLAS ARE HEARD AROUND THE WORLD

"I was with him the first day he walked on March 1, 1955 and I saw the deep wound in his back — you know that metal plate they had taken out — and I said that must hurt like hell and I'll never forget his reply — he said, 'I don't have to worry about pain. I don't have time to be here on my back. I'm going to be back in the Senate in a few months. There's only a short time for me to do everything that has to be done and I intend to do what has to be done or die trying.' I always wondered why he would say that in '55."

He had a premonition?

"Yes, but he had no fear of death. He thought that when he survived PT 109 and the back operation where he received the last rites of the church that he was indestructible. We talked about assassination. If someone wants to kill a president — I must have gone to Mass with him in different Catholic churches 100 times and I always thought that the nut that would want to kill him would do it in a Catholic church. But he said a high-powered rifle in a tall building, except it would be downtown with the confetti and the crowds would be so great and the noise so no one could point as they did in Dallas and say it came from up there."

He actually thought about it?

"Always — a high-powered rifle, telescope. He talked about it but he had no fear of it.

"I was in the car following, maybe 8–10 feet away and I heard the shots from behind. I was watching the President. But then I suddenly ducked, because I felt I heard shots from the side. I've always believed that there was more than one assassin."

DAVID F. POWERS

"At the time of the Cuban missile crisis last year, we discussed the possibility of war, a nuclear exchange, and talked about being killed — the latter at the time seemed so unimportant, almost frivolous. The one matter which . . . was of concern to President Kennedy and truly had meaning . . . was the specter of the death of the children of this country and around the world — the young people who had no part in and knew nothing of the confrontation, but whose lives would be snuffed out like anyone else's. They would never have been given a chance to make a decision, to vote in an election, to run for office, to lead a revolution, to determine their own destinies."

ROBERT F. KENNEDY

Covered with the American flag, the President's casket lies in the Capitol rotunda, with a long line of Americans paying their respects.

Overleaf: The funeral procession.

233

"The greatest leader of our time has been struck down by the foulest deed of our time. Today John Fitzgerald Kennedy lives on in the immortal words and works that he left behind. He lives on in the mind and memories of mankind. He lives on in the hearts of his countrymen.

"No words are sad enough to express our sense of loss. No words are strong enough to express our determination to continue the forward thrust of America that he began.

"The dream of conquering the vastness of space — the dream of partnership across the Atlantic — and across the Pacific as well — the dream of a Peace Corps in less developed nations — the dream of education for all of our children — the dream of jobs for all who seek them and need them — the dream of care for our elderly — the dream of an all-out attack on mental illness — and above all, the dream of equal rights for all Americans, whatever their race or color — these and other American dreams have been vitalized by his drive and by his dedication.

"And now the ideas and ideals which he so nobly represented must and will be translated into effective action."

LYNDON B. JOHNSON

"John F. Kennedy was so contemporary a man — so involved in our world, so immersed in our times, so responsive to its challenges, so intense a participant in the great events and decisions of our day — that he seemed the very symbol of the vitality and exuberance that is the essence of life itself."

ADLAI STEVENSON

"The loss to the United States and to the world is incalculable. Those who come after Mr. Kennedy must strive the more to achieve the ideals of world peace and human happiness and dignity to which his presidency was dedicated."

SIR WINSTON CHURCHILL

"President Kennedy died like a soldier, under fire, for his duty and in the service of his country."

CHARLES DE GAULLE

"I'll always remember the late President with deep respect because, in the final analysis, he showed himself to be sober-minded and determined to avoid war. He didn't let himself become frightened, nor did he become reckless. He didn't overestimate America's might, and he left himself a way out of the crisis. He showed real wisdom and statesmanship."

NIKITA KHRUSHCHEV

"The American people lose a truly major personality in their history and the peace-loving world a sincere champion of peace."

JOSIP TITO

"If I only had one gift, I think it is my faith. If I lost my wealth, or my looks, or my health, I could still accept the trials and tribulations which God has sent me because I trust in Him and He will never give me a cross heavier than I can bear."

ROSE KENNEDY

Presidium member Anastas Mikoyan and USSR Ambassador to Washington Anatoly Dobrynin at the graveside.

It may be he shall take my hand
And lead me into his dark land
And close my eyes and quench my breath . . .

But I've a rendezvous with Death
At midnight in some flaming town,
When spring trips north again this year,
And I to my pledged word am true,
I shall not fail that rendezvous.

ALAN SEEGER
"I Have a Rendezvous with Death"

This was one of the President's favourite poems. As a young Senator, he quoted it to his fiancée Jacqueline, who learned it by heart and quoted it back to him, always to his utter delight.

All generous hearts lament the leader killed,
    The young chief with the smile, the radiant face,
The winning way that turned a wondrous race
    Into sublimer pathways, leading on.

Grant to us Life that though the man be gone
    The promise of his spirit be fulfilled.

JOHN MASEFIELD
Poet Laureate of Great Britain
"John Fitzgerald Kennedy"

"Dear Lord
  Why did this have to be
  Why one so young
  Who put his faith and trust in Thee
  Why was it he?" . . .

AARON PAYNE
"I'll Remember"

. . . when he shall die,
    Take him and cut him out in little stars,
    And he will make the face of heaven so fine
    That all the world will be in love with night
    And pay no worship to the garish sun.

WILLIAM SHAKESPEARE
Romeo and Juliet

Robert F. Kennedy's words on introducing a film on John F. Kennedy during the 1964 Democratic Convention. The demonstration in response lasted for twenty-two minutes, with many unable to hold back their tears.

Mourners at Arlington Cemetery.

JOHN F. KENNEDY, 'In Memoriam'

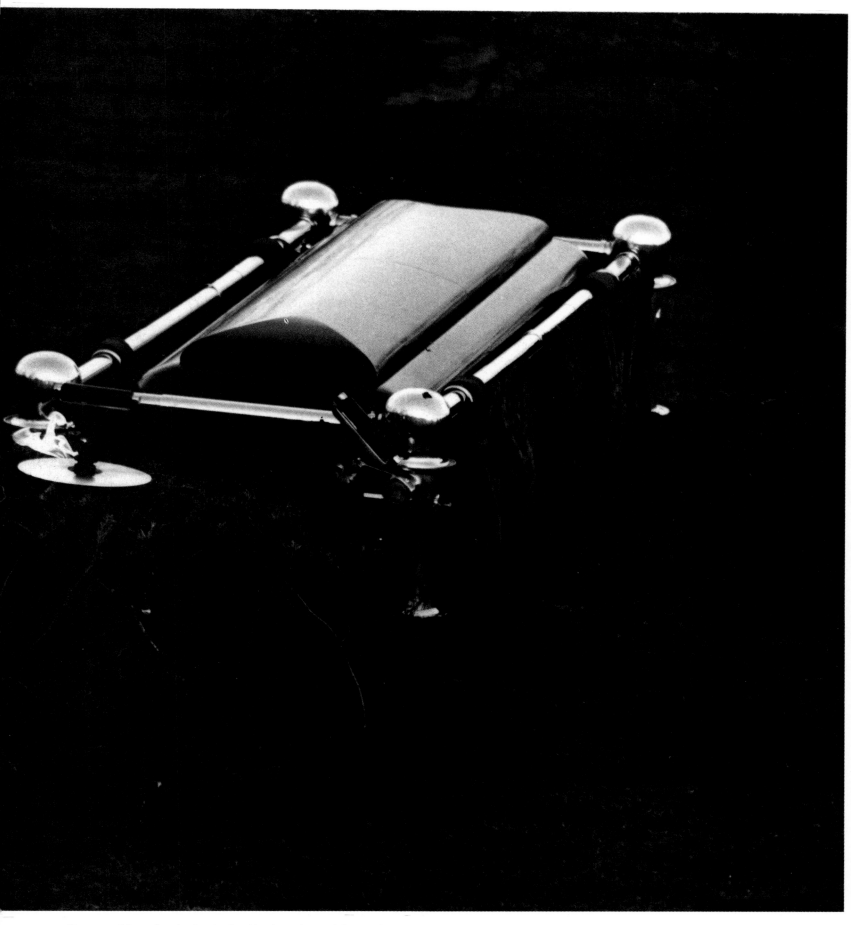

The eternal flame burning by the President's casket at Arlington Cemetery.

BEFORE THE STORM

Lyndon Johnson is elected and Bobby Runs for the Senate

President Lyndon B. Johnson campaigning.

Continuity at the White House. Kennedy aides Pierre Salinger (left) and Ted Sorensen (sitting) conferring with the President together with Johnson aides Bill Moyers and Jack Valenti (background).

"I do solemnly swear that I will faithfully execute the office of President of the United States and will, to the best of my ability, preserve, protect and defend the constitution of the United States, so help me God."

LYNDON B. JOHNSON

The oath of office, administered by Judge Sarah Hughes aboard *Airforce I* sitting on the tarmac in Dallas, Texas

President Johnson and Lady Bird in the private quarters at the White House. Later in his book *The Vantage Point,* he says, "I had decidedly mixed feelings about whether I wanted to seek a four-year term." Lady Bird, in a memo weighing the risks, difficulties and the strain of the presidency, nevertheless came out strongly in favour of his running, ending her memo: "Stay in. Realize it's going to be rough — but remember we worry much in advance about troubles that never happen! Pace yourself, within the limits of your personality. If you lose in November — it's all settled anyway. If you win, let's do the best we can for three years and three or four months — and then, the Lord letting us live that long, announce in February or March 1968 that you are not a candidate for re-election. You'll then be fifty-nine, and by the end of that term a mellow sixty, and I believe the juices of life will be stilled enough to let you come home in relative peace and acceptance (we may even have grandchildren). Your loving wife."

The new President moved swiftly in completing the unfinished business of the Kennedy administration. He was a compassionate man, he had seen poverty in his youth and understood people's suffering. A Southerner, he also had a feeling of kinship with the plight of the Negro and sympathy with the civil rights struggle. His concerns extended to the problems of the elderly, as expressed in the Medicare programme, and to the plight of the young, as expressed in the Job Corps bill and education bills. A superb parliamentarian, he understood the workings of the Congress better than any other man, and as the long-time Senate Majority Leader, he knew how to get bills passed, how to motivate the legislators, better than President Kennedy had known. And the results were astonishing. Defying Republicans, his own Southern brethren and conservatives in general, a comprehensive civil rights bill was passed, poverty bills were signed and a flood of bills emanated from the White House, with a docile Congress hardly demurring. Considered a conservative by labour, by the blacks, by the poor and by the civil libertarians, he became their hero. His style might not have been that of his predecessor, he didn't inspire the nation as Kennedy had done, but he got things done on the side of the angels. And then it all stopped. More and more he became mired in the war in Vietnam, obsessed with it. Where Kennedy had little use for the military, Johnson trusted them implicitly. And as the war escalated to ever grimmer heights and the country became an armed camp of dissent and counter-dissent, the compassion he had showed in his first days in office, the concerns he had brought to the presidency, were put on the back burner. There were other priorities now. It would finally destroy him and lose him his rightful place in history.

"... Let this session of Congress be known as the session which did more for civil rights than the last hundred sessions combined ... as the session which declared all-out war on human poverty and unemployment in these United States ... as the session which finally recognized the health needs of all our older citizens ... and as the session which helped to build more homes, more schools, more libraries, and more hospitals than any single session of Congress in the history of the Republic ... Let us carry forward the plans and programs of John Fitzgerald Kennedy — not because of our sorrow or sympathy, but because they are right ... Unfortunately, many Americans live on the outskirts of hope — some because of their poverty, and some because of their color, and all too many because of both ... This administration today ... declares unconditional war on poverty in America ... It will not be a short or easy struggle ... but we shall not rest until the war is won ... We cannot afford to lose it ... (but) pursue it in city slums and small towns, in sharecropper shacks or in migrant worker camps, on Indian reservations, among whites as well as Negroes, among the young as well as the aged ... No single piece of legislation is going to suffice ... We will launch a special effort in the chronically distressed areas of Appalachia ... We must enact youth employment legislation to put jobless, aimless, hopeless youngsters to work ... We must distribute more food to the needy ... We must create a National Service Corps ... We must extend the coverage of our minimum wage laws ... We must ... improve the quality of teaching ... We must build more libraries ... more hospitals and nursing homes ... and train more nurses to staff them ... All of these increased opportunities ... must be open to Americans of every color ... we must abolish not some, but all racial discrimination. For this is not merely an economic issue ... It is a moral issue ... our ultimate goal is a world without war, a world made safe for diversity ... In 1964 we will be better prepared than ever before to defend the cause of freedom ... and we shall make new proposals ... toward the control and the eventual abolition of arms ... We must make increased use of our food as an instrument of peace ... we must expand world trade ... we must strengthen the ability of free nations everywhere to develop their independence and raise their standard of living ... To do this, the rich must help the poor — and we must do our part ... we must develop with our allies new means of bridging the gap between the East and the West ... In these last seven sorrowful weeks, we have learned anew that nothing is so enduring as faith, and nothing is so degrading as hate ... John Kennedy was a victim of hate, but he was also a great builder of faith ... So I ask you now ... to join me in working for a nation that is free from want and a world that is free from hate — a world of peace and justice, and freedom and abundance, for our time and for all time to come."
LYNDON B. JOHNSON
State of the Union, January 8, 1964

Left, top: Following ratification of the Voting Rights amendment to the Constitution, which abolished the poll tax, a tax which had been used to keep blacks from voting, especially in the South, black registration increased sharply, resulting in the election of blacks as Mayor, Sheriff and to countless other effective offices. *Left:* President Johnson at his LBJ ranch in Texas with military and civilian advisers early in 1964.

"I have no presidential ambitions, nor does my wife Ethel."
ROBERT F. KENNEDY

Robert F. Kennedy in his successful, yet difficult, quest for the New York State Senate seat, addresses a crowd on Wall Street estimated at 500,000. He had offered his services as Ambassador to Saigon; Johnson had turned him down. He had actively sought the vice-presidential spot for the 1964 election and Johnson had declared Cabinet members ineligible. Bobby had had no other place to go and had accepted the carpetbagging accusations. He won, but he was not content.

"I have decided to make myself available for the nomination of the Democratic State Convention. I have made that decision because I think our country faces a fundamental, political choice."
ROBERT F. KENNEDY

"You don't very often find a person that has the understanding and the ability and the heart — the compassion that Bob Kennedy has."
LYNDON B. JOHNSON

"He was a carpetbagger in the minds of a lot of people. He was arrogant in the minds of a lot of people and he fundamentally had trouble for those two reasons with a large sector of the vote in NY."
CHARLES GUGGENHEIM

"You know as I was touring upstate I kept seeing the signs saying 'go back home' — 'carpet bagger go home' — and now here I am."
ROBERT F. KENNEDY

Walt Rostow, Dean Rusk and President Lyndon B. Johnson in the Oval Office at the White House. Somehow the photograph evokes the utter hopelessness and tragedy of a President lost, mired in divisive policies that could not be undone. Johnson would bury his Republican opponent, Barry Goldwater, in a victory not equalled since Franklin Roosevelt's election over Alf Landon in 1936, but the end was already in sight. Moreover, Johnson would win on a "peace" platform, but it was war that would destroy him in the forthcoming term.

"In reference to the selection of a candidate for vice president on the Democratic ticket, I have reached the conclusion that it would be inadvisable for me to recommend to the convention any member of the Cabinet . . ."

LYNDON B. JOHNSON

"These are the stakes: to make a world in which all of God's children can live, or to go into the dark. Either we must love each other or we must die."

Television commercial for President Johnson's election campaign. The visual showed a little girl counting to ten, which dissolved into a countdown for an atomic explosion. It was in answer to Goldwater's threat to defoliate Vietnam. The effect of the commercial was instant and devastating.

DARKEST HOURS

Vietnam Divides the Nation · The Death of Martin Luther King Jr.

". . . renewed hostile actions against United States ships on the high seas in the Gulf of Tonkin have today required me to order the military forces of the United States to take action in reply.

"The initial attack on the destroyer Maddox . . . was repeated today by a number of hostile vessels attacking two US destroyers with torpedoes. The destroyers and supporting aircraft acted at once on the orders I gave . . . We believe at least two of the attacking boats were sunk. There were no US losses . . .

". . . repeated acts of violence against the Armed Forces of the United States must be met not only with alert defense, but with positive reply . . . Air action is now in execution against gunboats and certain supporting facilities in North Vietnam which have been used in these hostile operations . . .

"Aggression by terror against the peaceful villagers of South Vietnam has now been joined by open aggression on the high seas against the United States of America . . .

"We Americans know, although others appear to forget, the risks of spreading conflict. We still seek no wider war . . .

"I have today met with the leaders of both parties in the Congress of the United States, and I have informed them that I shall immediately request the Congress to pass a resolution making it clear that our government is united in its determination to take all necessary measures in support of freedom and in defense of peace in Southeast Asia . . ."

LYNDON B. JOHNSON
Request for Gulf of Tonkin Resolution, August 4, 1964

Pro-war demonstrator in New York.

"As we phase out the Old Year and welcome the New Year, we do so with the confidence that what we Americans are fighting for in Vietnam is right — and that God has always been on the side of those who are right. The voices of dissension have risen many times throughout the land — but they have not spoken for the majority of the people — and they have not prevailed. We can look back with pride on another year of slow but steady progress in the long struggle we and our Vietnamese allies have engaged in to bring a just and honorable peace to this land.

"And looking back over the sacrifices that so many Americans have made here — sacrifices that I have personally observed in my five years in Vietnam — I am even more proud to say — I am an American. And I believe that we must rededicate ourselves to the effort that will bring the final victory and ask ourselves — what is it about this great country of ours — these United States of America — that has inspired brave men to fight and die for her for so many years in order to preserve her freedom."

JOHN VIRGIL SWANGO
Province Senior Adviser, Chau Doc Province

Anti-war student demonstrations (above) in Washington, DC and (below) at San Francisco State College, California. The country's values had been shattered, its morality mortally wounded.

Come on all of you big
   strong men
Uncle Sam needs your help
   again.
He's got himself in a terrible
   jam
Way down yonder in
   Vietnam.
So put down your books,
   pick up a gun
We're gonna have a whole
   lot of fun.
It's one, two, three, what
   are we fighting for?
Don't ask me, I don't give a
   damn,
Next stop is Vietnam.
. . .
Be the first one on the block
To have your boy come
   home in a box.
   ''I Feel Like I'm Fixing to Die Rag''

Words and music by
COUNTRY JOE McDONALD

Key foreign affairs advisers meet with President Johnson for the regular Tuesday luncheon.

*"If I had to pick a date that symbolized the turmoil
we experienced throughout 1968, I think
January 23 would be the day . . .
the morning the USS Pueblo was
seized . . . It formed the first link in a chain that
added up to one of the most agonizing years any
president has ever spent in the White House."*

LYNDON B. JOHNSON

General Westmoreland (centre) in Saigon.

How far is it
from Guernica to Man Quang
from Washington to Berchtesgaden
from Munich to Prague
from Berlin to Moscow
to Warsaw?

How far was it
from Guernica to Munich?
one year and five months
That is not very far
How far was it
from Guernica to Warsaw
from Hitler to whom
and to what country?

From Saigon to Hanoi as far
as from Berlin to Belgrade
or from Manchester down to
    Guernica
I looked for Guernica on the map of
    Spain
because I had no other way
of seeing Man Quang

What have the schoolchildren of
    Man Quang
learned from the bombs?
What have we learned
from the schoolchildren of Man
    Quang?
What have we learned
from Guernica and from Poland
from Coventry Stalingrad Dresden
Nagasaki Suez Sakiet?

That it isn't all that far
or that it hasn't got that far yet
or that things can never
get that far?
The parents picked up the children
in their coffins
and carried them
to the foreign soldiers

They were beaten back by the
    soldiers
and they carried the coffins back to
    Man Quang

ERICH FRIED
"Schoolchildren"

The Eastern world, it is
    explodin'.
Violence flarin' and bullets
    loadin',
You're old enough to kill, but not
    for votin',
You don't believe in war, but
    what's that gun you're totin'?
And even the Jordan River has
    bodies floatin'!
But you tell me over and over
    and over again my friend,
Ah, you don't believe we're on
    the eve of destruction.

Don't you understand what I'm
    tryin' to say?
Can't you feel the fear that I'm
    feelin' today?
If the button is pushed there's
    no running away
There'll be no one to save with
    the world in a grave.
Take a look around you, boy, it's
    bound to scare you, boy,
But you . . . don't believe we're
    on the eve of destruction.
    "The Eve of Destruction"
Words and music by P.F. SLOAN and STEVE BARRI
    Recorded by BARRY McGUIRE

*"I'm opposed to resuming
    the bombing at the
    moment until I have
information that indicates
    that such resumption is
    necessary or is in our
    national interest."*
    ROBERT F. KENNEDY

We shall overcome,
We shall overcome,
We shall overcome some day,
Oh, deep in my heart
I do believe
We shall overcome some day.

We'll walk hand in hand,
We'll walk hand in hand,
We'll walk hand in hand some
    day,
Oh, deep in my heart
I do believe
We shall overcome some day.

We are not afraid,
We are not afraid,
We are not afraid today,
Oh, deep in my heart
I do believe
We shall overcome some day.

We shall stand together,
We shall stand together,
We shall stand together — now,
Oh, deep in my heart
I do believe
We shall overcome some day.

''We Shall Overcome''
Words and music adapted by
ZILPHIA HORTON, FRANK HAMILTON,
GUY CARAWAN and PETE SEEGER

Freedom marchers, Selma, Alabama.

A sheriff's posse.

"At this point he went through what (Abraham) Lincoln went through. Lincoln had real agonizing moments over this question of signing the Emancipation Proclamation, as you know. He vacillated a great deal. But finally, the events caused him to see that he had to do this, and he came to the moral conclusion that he had to do it no matter what it meant. I think Kennedy was just at this point . . . He brought to the presidency a moral concern for the issue of civil rights and placed before the national public the principle that the civil rights issue was a moral issue . . . His speech last summer I think is the most eloquent, passionate, and unequivocal plea for civil rights, for justice toward the Negro ever made by any president, and this came on the heels of the Birmingham movement."

MARTIN LUTHER KING JR.

"You are asking today, 'How long will it take?' It will not be long. How long? Not long, because no lie can live forever. How long? Not long, because you still reap what you sow. How long? Not long, because mine eyes have seen the glory of the coming of the Lord. He is trampling out the vintage where the grapes of wrath are stored. He has loosed the fateful lightning of his terrible swift sword. His truth is marching on . . . Oh, be swift, my soul, to answer Him. Be jubiliant, my feet. Our God is marching on.
Glory, glory hallelujah!
Glory, glory hallelujah!
Glory, glory hallelujah!"

MARTIN LUTHER KING JR.

The Death of Martin Luther King Jr.

On the night of the death of Martin Luther King Jr., Robert Kennedy fulfilled a speaking engagement in the ghetto of Indianapolis. The area was considered dangerous when King was alive; now, even the police escort left the candidate at the edge of the ghetto. Robert Kennedy was perhaps the only white man in America able to confront that audience on that night, and stay alive.

"I have bad news for you, for all of our fellow citizens, and people who love peace all over the world, and that is that Martin Luther King was shot and killed tonight . . . For those of you who are black and are tempted to be filled with hatred and distrust . . . against all white people, I can only say that I feel in my own heart the same kind of feeling . . ."

ROBERT F. KENNEDY

There were riots in 110 cities, 39 people were killed and more than 2500 injured.

Coretta Scott King at her husband's funeral. The assassination of Martin Luther King Jr. shocked the nation as much as John Kennedy's assassination had shocked all of America and the world. Ask any black and he can tell you what he was doing at the time, as half the world can of the Kennedy assassination. Once again, a moderate man, a man of peace, a visionary leader, a prophet who had followed the "non-violent protest" teachings of Mahatma Gandhi, had been mowed down by the anger and violence which had by now become part of the American character, it seemed. He was unafraid, expecting his fate, and his death was an incalculable tragedy. Mourners came from everywhere, black and white, Catholic and Protestant, rich and poor, and a crowd estimated at nearly 100,000 surrounded his own Ebenezer Baptist Church during the memorial service. Two mules pulled his simple casket on a rickety farm cart to his grave, surrounded by a guard of honour of black leaders and followed by a crowd which stretched beyond the horizon.

"If any of you are around when I have to meet my day I don't want a long speech. I'd like somebody to mention that day that Martin Luther King, Jr., tried to give his life for others. I'd like somebody to say that day that Martin Luther King, Jr., tried to love somebody . . . I won't have any money to leave behind. I won't have the fine and luxurious things of life to leave behind. But I just want to leave a committed life behind. Then my living will not be in vain."

MARTIN LUTHER KING JR.

"Well, I don't know what will happen now. We've got some difficult days ahead. But it doesn't matter with me now. Because I've been to the mountaintop. And I don't mind. Like anybody, I would like to live a long life. Longevity has its place. But I'm not concerned about that now. I just want to do God's will. And He's allowed me to go up to the mountain. And I've looked over. And I've seen the promised land. I may not get there with you. But I want you to know tonight, that we as a people will get to the promised land. And I'm happy, tonight. I'm not worried about anything. I'm not fearing any man. Mine eyes have seen the glory of the coming of the Lord."

MARTIN LUTHER KING JR., "I've Been to the Mountaintop"

PICKING UP THE TORCH

Bobby Kennedy in His Run for President Becomes the Hope of the
Young, the Poor, the Underprivileged

"The thing I feared from the first day of my presidency was actually coming true. Robert Kennedy has openly announced his intention to reclaim the throne in the memory of his brother."

LYNDON B. JOHNSON to Doris Kearns

The night before Robert Kennedy announced his intention to run for the presidency there was a party for newspaper editors at Hickory Hill.

"I remember it being rather awkward because President Johnson called him six times that night. And the butler kept coming in and saying President Johnson's on the phone instead of whispering it. He just said it to our table but it was enough to make everybody sort of unsettled. And then I remember during the next few days the different editors calling and saying weren't we dumb not to know what was going on."

ETHEL KENNEDY

Eugene McCarthy speaking to a rally.

"I had a fear that the Kennedys were a sort of intrusion, that they were going to capture the party and make it into their own instrument which in fact they did — the party has not recovered from that since."

EUGENE McCARTHY

First strategy conference at Hickory Hill on the forthcoming presidential campaign. Two generations of Kennedy advisers are present, including Sorensen, O'Donnell, Salinger of John F. Kennedy's staff and Mankiewicz, Walinsky, Edelman of Robert F. Kennedy's staff, all joined now, ready to fight another battle.

"I think much more to the point was President Johnson — they had a meeting in 1967 in which President Johnson said flatly and openly, in six months you and all the people who think like you are going to be destroyed. And I'm sure that when a sitting president and one as powerful as Lyndon Johnson makes such a threat you pay attention and you are right to pay attention when you represent what Robert Kennedy did."
ADAM WALINSKY

Brother-in-law Steve Smith and Senator Ted Kennedy at the meeting.

The Kennedy spirit is definitely intact and alive.

"I'd like to harness all the energy and effort and incentive and imagination that was attracted to government by President Kennedy. I don't want any of that to die . . . if I could figure out some course for me that would keep all that alive and utilize it for the country, that is what I would do."

ROBERT F. KENNEDY

Robert Kennedy campaigning for the presidency.

"I shall not seek, and I shall not accept the nomination of my party for another term as your President."
LYNDON B. JOHNSON

"Those men responsible for our present course — those who have removed themselves from the American tradition, from the enduring and generous impulses that are the soul of this nation. They are the ones who divide this country."
ROBERT F. KENNEDY

"What we need in the United States is not division; what we need in the United States is not hatred; what we need in the United States is not violence or lawlessness, but love and wisdom, and compassion toward one another; and a feeling of justice toward those who still suffer within our country . . ."
ROBERT F. KENNEDY

"We loved him so much . . . For every man working for John Kennedy we must have had about fifty men working for Bobby. It was electrifying . . . It was respect, admiration, love . . . it was a phenomenon that can't be explained . . . there was a 100 per cent turnout for (Bob) Kennedy . . . Who's going to fill that vacuum?"
CESAR CHAVEZ

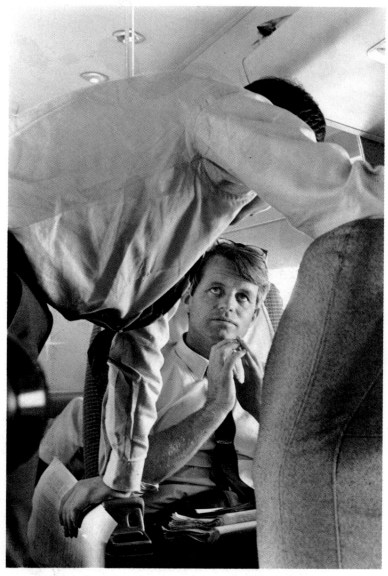

Robert F. Kennedy in his campaign plane.

Cesar Chavez demonstrating in California.

"The most powerful country the world has known now turns its strength and will upon a small and primitive land . . . a land deafened by the unending crescendo of violence, hatred and savage fury . . . It is we who live in abundance and send our young men out to die . . . We are not in Vietnam to play the role of an avenging angel pouring death and destruction on the roads and factories and homes of a guilty land. We are there to assure the self-determination of South Vietnam . . ."

ROBERT F. KENNEDY
Address to the Senate on the bombing in Vietnam

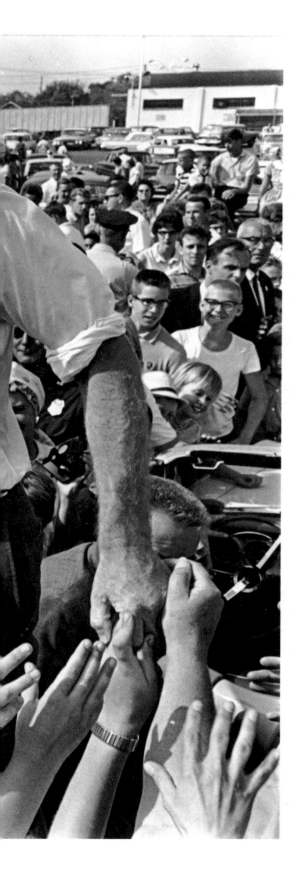

"All these places — Harlem, Watts, Southside — are riots waiting to happen."
ROBERT F. KENNEDY

"We loved him too, Mrs. Kennedy. Loving a public official for an Indian is almost unheard of, as history bears out. We trusted him. Unheard of too, for an Indian. We had faith in him."
Letter from a Seneca Indian to Ethel Kennedy

"Tears were running down (Kennedy's) cheeks and he just sat there and held the little child. Roaches and rats were all over the floor. Then he said 'I'm going back to Washington to do something about this.' No other white man in America would have come into that house."
CHARLES EVERS
On visiting a black ghetto with Robert Kennedy

"What the hell would you do if you found out that God was black?"
ROBERT F. KENNEDY
Talking to Afrikaner students at Stellenbosch University in South Africa

"Give me your help, you give me your help in the next three months and we win the primary here in the state of California, we'll win in Chicago in August, we'll win the election in November and we'll have a new country, a new state of California and we'll make a new day for mankind with your help. Thank you very much."
ROBERT F. KENNEDY

DEATH IN LOS ANGELES

The Second Brother is Slain

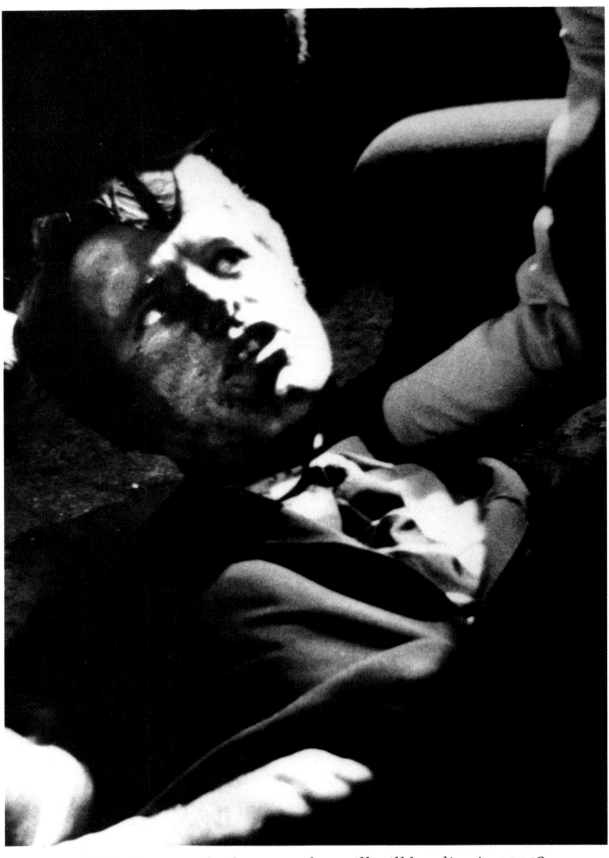

*"Who knows whether any of us will still be alive in 1972?
Existence is so fickle, Fate is so fickle."*
ROBERT F. KENNEDY

"It is better to light
A candle
Then to curse the
darkness."
LAO TZE

We are deeply grateful to you for remembering us
in your thoughts and your prayers

We that had loved him so, followed him, honored him,
lived in his mild and magnificent eye,
learned his great language, caught his clear accents,
made him our pattern to live and to die.

Robert Browning, "The Lost Leader"

Senator and Mrs. Edward M. Kennedy

COLOUR PLATE CAPTIONS

i   Joseph P. Kennedy and Caroline at his Hyannis Port house. Summer 1958.

ii   Jacqueline and John F. Kennedy with Caroline at Hyannis Port shortly before the Senator's re-election victory in 1958.

iii   At the same sitting as the photograph on the left.

iv   Robert F. Kennedy and Ethel at Hickory Hill with, from left, David, Kathleen, Joe, Michael, Mary Courtney and Bobby. 1959.

v   The first and most used campaign poster. This was based on a photograph taken in Nebraska, which was later used for several primary campaign posters and brochure covers and finally served as the 'In Memoriam' card.

vi   Campaigning in Wisconsin. To Kennedy's right sits Governor Gaylord Nelson. The photograph in the background was from our first and difficult sitting.

vii   Senator Kennedy accepts the Democratic presidential nomination. It was here that he announced the New Frontier.

viii   Portrait taken at the Democratic Convention, 1960.

ix   The first formal portrait of the President in the Oval Office. February 1961.

x   Robert F. Kennedy in his library at Hickory Hill. Autumn 1961.

xi   Jacqueline Kennedy at her house in Hyannis Port. Summer 1960, shortly after the Democratic Convention.

xii   Jacqueline, Caroline and Senator Kennedy after the Democratic Convention at Hyannis Port. Summer 1960.

xiii   Caroline and Jacqueline Kennedy at the Senator's house in Hyannis Port. Summer 1960.

xiv   The Robert Kennedy family again at Hickory Hill. The new addition is Mary Kerry, second from the left. Autumn 1961.

xv   David Kennedy and Maria Shriver playing in the sand in front of Joseph P. Kennedy's house, the Big House. The house in the background, on the left is Robert Kennedy's. The house on the far left is John F. Kennedy's.

xvi   A painting by Jacqueline Kennedy, presented as a birthday present to her father-in-law, depicts the Kennedy compound with Nurse Shaw in the background, Caroline running, John F. Kennedy carrying a golfclub, Jacqueline in a bathing suit carrying flippers and Joseph P. Kennedy at the right in the foreground watching the scene. The inscription reads "To Grandpa, love, Jackie".

SOURCES

GOVERNOR ROSS BARNETT
   John Fitzgerald Kennedy Library Oral History Project (p.176)
LeMOYNE BILLINGS
   John Fitzgerald Kennedy . . . As We Remember Him edited by Goddard Lieberson (p.34)
CESAR CHAVEZ
   John Fitzgerald Kennedy Library Oral History Project (p.263)
SIR WINSTON CHURCHILL
   John F. Kennedy by Urs Schwartz (p.236)
CHARLES DE GAULLE
   John Fitzgerald Kennedy by Urs Schwartz (p.236)
   Public Papers of the Presidents (p.192)
WILLIAM O. DOUGLAS
   John Fitzgerald Kennedy Library Oral History Project (p.161)
KAY EVANS
   American Journey, the Times of Robert Kennedy, Interviews by Jean Stein edited by George Plimpton (p.216)
CHARLES EVERS
   Robert Kennedy and His Times by Arthur M. Schlesinger (p.264)
ERICH FRIED
   "Schoolchildren" poem from *Und Vietnam und 41 Gedichte* (p.252)
CHARLES GUGGENHEIM
   BBC TV transcript "Reputations: Robert Kennedy" (p.246)
HUBERT H. HUMPHREY
   The Making of the President 1960 by Theodore H. White (p.67)
LYNDON BAINES JOHNSON
   Acceptance Speech as vice-presidential candidate July 15, 1960 (p.108)
   Public Papers of the Presidents (pp.236, 243, 245, 247, 248)
   Quoted from *The Vantage Point* (pp.243, 252)
   Lyndon Johnson and the American Dream by Doris Kearns (p.259)
   Excerpt from Lyndon Johnson's statement on his withdrawing from the presidential race (p.263)
NICHOLAS KATZENBACH
   BBC TV transcript "Reputations: Robert Kennedy" (p.159)
ETHEL KENNEDY
   BBC TV transcript "Reputations: Robert Kennedy" (pp.158, 259)
JACQUELINE KENNEDY
   Portrait: The Emergence of John F Kennedy by Jacques Lowe (p.55)
   Letter to the author (p.61)
   John Fitzgerald Kennedy . . . As We Remember Him edited by Goddard Lieberson (p.62)
   Jacqueline Kennedy, First Lady by Jacques Lowe (pp.74, 220, 229)
   Lyndon Baines Johnson Library Oral History Project (p.226)
   A Thousand Days by Arthur M. Schlesinger (p.227)
JOHN F. KENNEDY
   (Where no specific source is mentioned the quotations have been taken from campaign speeches)
   Times to Remember by Rose Fitzgerald Kennedy (p.11)
   Why England Slept by John F. Kennedy (p.41)
   Hyannis Armory, remarks to the Press Monday January 9, 1960 (p.125)
   "Citizens for Kennedy and Johnson" campaign literature (p.47)
   Congressional Record (pp.54, 58, 68)

Interview with the *New York Times* (p.58)
   Johnny We Hardly Knew Ye by Kenneth O'Donnell and David F. Powers with Joe McCarthy (p.77)
   More Kennedy Wit by Bill Adler (pp.81, 83, 185)
   Senator John F. Kennedy writing in *Look* magazine (pp.92, 93, 94, 95, 96, 98)
   Public Papers (pp.135, 145, 157, 167, 168, 172, 174, 175, 178, 189, 195, 202, 203, 204, 205, 207)
   A Thousand Days by Arthur M. Schlesinger Jr. (pp.161, 208)
   Remarks at dinner honouring Nobel Prizewinners of the Western Hemisphere April 29, 1962 (p.174)
   Toast to André Malraux, French Minister for Cultural Affairs at the White House May 11, 1962 (p.175)
   John F. Kennedy by Urs Schwartz (p.177)
   From a CBS tape (p.226)
JOSEPH P. KENNEDY
   The Remarkable Kennedys by Joe McCarthy (pp.18, 19)
   Interview in the *Boston Globe* (p.41)
ROBERT F. KENNEDY
   BBC TV transcript "Reputations: Robert Kennedy" (pp.11, 38, 261, 263)
   John F. Kennedy by Urs Schwartz (p.177)
   Thirteen Days (pp.180–1)
   John Fitzgerald Kennedy . . . As We Remember Him edited by Goddard Lieberson (p.232)
   Robert Kennedy and His Times by Arthur M. Schlesinger (pp.246, 264)
   Excerpt from Robert Kennedy's announcement to run for the New York Senate seat (p.246)
   Excerpt from a campaign speech (p.246)
   Indianapolis April 4, 1968 in the black ghetto on the night of Martin Luther King Jr.'s assassination (p.263)
   Congressional Record (p.264)
   Senate speech on bombing in Vietnam March 2, 1967 (p.265)
ROSE FITZGERALD KENNEDY
   Times to Remember (pp.14, 17, 19, 30–1, 34, 36)
   Rose – a film produced by the Kennedy family (pp.21, 24, 34, 236)
   John Fitzgerald Kennedy . . . As We Remember Him edited by Goddard Lieberson (pp.23, 27)
NIKITA KHRUSHCHEV
   Khrushchev Remembers (pp.179, 194, 236)
MARTIN LUTHER KING JR.
   John Fitzgerald Kennedy Library Oral History Project (p.255)
   Last sermon of Martin Luther King at the Ebenezer Baptist Church. The tape was played at the funeral service (p.256)
WALTER LIPPMAN
   Newsweek January 21, 1963 (p.148)
JACQUES LOWE
   Portrait: The Emergence of John F. Kennedy (p.123)
HENRY R. LUCE
   John Fitzgerald Kennedy Library Oral History Project (pp.41, 165)
EUGENE McCARTHY
   BBC TV transcript "Reputations: Robert Kennedy" (p.259)
TORBERT MACDONALD
   John Fitzgerald Kennedy . . . As We Remember Him edited by Goddard Lieberson (p.211)

HAROLD MACMILLAN
   At the End of the Day by Harold Macmillan (p.171)
JAMES McSHANE
   John Fitzgerald Kennedy Library Oral History Project (p.98)
JACK NEWFIELD
   BBC TV transcript "Reputations: Robert Kennedy" (p.159)
KENNETH O'DONNELL
   Johnny We Hardly Knew Ye (p.67)
DAVID F. POWERS
   Interviews with the author (pp.51, 53, 87, 109, 120, 212, 221, 232)
   John Fitzgerald Kennedy . . . As We Remember Him edited by
   Goddard Lieberson (p.207)
MARY KENNEDY RYAN
   John Fitzgerald Kennedy . . . As We Remember Him edited by
   Goddard Lieberson (p.206)
ARTHUR SCHLESINGER JR.
   A Thousand Days (p.227)
ALAN SEEGER
   "I Have a Rendezvous with Death" A.M.S. Press, New York (p.238)

EUNICE SHRIVER
   Jacqueline Kennedy: First Lady by Jacques Lowe (p.209)
CHARLES SPAULDING
   John Fitzgerald Kennedy . . . As We Remember Him edited by
   Goddard Lieberson (p.45)
GEORGE STEVENS
   *American Journey, the Times of Robert Kennedy, Interviews by Jean
   Stein* edited by George Plimpton (p.219)
ADLAI STEVENSON
   John F. Kennedy by Urs Schwartz (p.236)
JOHN VIRGIL SWANGO
   Vietnam Inc. by Philip Jones Griffiths (p.250)
JOSIP TITO
   John F. Kennedy by Urs Schwartz (p.236)
ADAM WALINSKY
   BBC TV transcript "Reputations: Robert Kennedy" (p.260)
JIM WHITTAKER
   *American Journey, the Times of Robert Kennedy, Interviews by Jean
   Stein* edited by George Plimpton (p.230)

BIBLIOGRAPHY

Adler, Bill (editor), *The Kennedy Wit*. The Citadel Press, 1964.
Adler, Bill (editor), *More Kennedy Wit*. The Citadel Press, 1965.
Bradlee, Benjamin C., *That Special Grace*. Lippincott, 1964.
Bradlee, Benjamin C., *Conversations with Kennedy*. W.W. Norton & Co.,
      1975.
Burns, James MacGregor, *John Kennedy*. Harcourt Brace & World,
      1961.
Fried, Erich, *Und Vietnam und 41 Gedichte*. Verlag Klaus, Wagenbach,
      1966.
Frost, Robert, *Poetry and Prose,* edited by Edward Connery Lathem. Holt
      Rinehart & Winston, 1972.
Frost, Robert, *North of Boston,* edited by Edward Connery Lathem. Dodd
      Mead & Company, 1977.
Frost, Robert, *The Poetry of Robert Frost,* edited by Edward Connery
      Lathem. Jonathan Cape Ltd, 1977.
Frost, Robert, *In the Clearing*. Holt Rinehart & Winston, 1979.
Gardner, Gerald (editor), *The Shining Moments*. Pocket Books Inc., 1964.
Goldman, Eric F., *The Tragedy of Lyndon Johnson*. Alfred A. Knopf Inc.,
      1968/69.
Griffiths, Philip Jones, *Vietnam Inc.* Collier Books, 1971.
Halberstam, David, *The Unfinished Odyssey of Robert F. Kennedy*.
      Random House Inc., 1968.
Herr, Michael, *Dispatches*. Alfred A. Knopf Inc., 1977.
Johnson, Lyndon B., *Public Papers of the Presidents*. U.S. Government
      Printing Office, 1963, 1964, 1965, 1966, 1967,
      1968.
Johnson, Lyndon B., *The Vantage Point*. Holt Rinehart & Winston, 1971.
Kaiser, Robert Blair, *"RFK Must Die!"* E.P. Dutton & Co., 1970.
Kearns, Doris, *Lyndon Johnson and the American Dream*. Andre
      Deutsch, 1976.
Kennedy, John F., *Profiles in Courage*. Harper & Bros., 1955/56.
Kennedy, John F., *The Strategy of Peace*. Harper & Bros., 1960.
Kennedy, John F., *Public Papers of the Presidents*. U.S. Government
      Printing Office, 1961, 1962, 1963.
Kennedy, John F., *Why England Slept*. Wilfred Funk Inc., 1961.
Kennedy, Robert F., *The Enemy Within*. Harper & Bros., 1960.
Kennedy, Robert F., *To Seek a Newer World*. Doubleday, 1967.
Kennedy, Robert F., *Thirteen Days*. W.W. Norton & Co., 1971.
Kennedy, Rose Fitzgerald, *Times to Remember*. Doubleday, 1974.
Khrushchev, Nikita, *Khrushchev Remembers*. Introduction,
      Commentary and Notes by Edward Crankshaw.
      Translated and edited by Strobe Talbott. Little,
      Brown & Co., 1970.
Lash, Joseph P., *Eleanor. The Years Alone*. W.W. Norton & Co., 1972.
Lieberson, Goddard (editor), *John Fitzgerald Kennedy . . . As We
      Remember Him*. Atheneum, 1965.
Lowe, Jacques/The *New York Times, The Kennedy Years*. The Viking
      Press, 1964.
Lowe, Jacques, *Portrait. The Emergence of John F. Kennedy*. McGraw
      Hill, 1961.
McCarthy, Joe, *The Remarkable Kennedys*. Popular Library Edition,
      1960.
Macmillan, Harold, *At the End of the Day*. Macmillan, 1973.
Manchester, William, *The Death of a President*. Michael Joseph, 1967.
Miller, Merle, *Lyndon. An Oral Biography*. G.P. Putnam's Sons, 1980.
Neustadt, Richard E., *Presidential Power*. John Wiley & Sons, Inc., 1960.

Newfield, Jack, *Robert Kennedy. A Memoir*. E.P. Dutton & Co., 1969.
O'Donnell, Kenneth P. and David F. Powers with Joe McCarthy, *Johnny
      We Hardly Knew Ye*. Little, Brown & Co., 1972.
Oral History Project of the John F. Kennedy Library
      Barnett, Ross   May 6, 1969
      Chavez, Cesar   January 28, 1970
      Douglas, William O.   November 9, 1967
      Glenn, John   June 12, 1964
      Khrushchev, Nikita
      King, Martin Luther, Jr.   March 9, 1964
      Luce, Henry   November 11, 1965
      McShane, James P.   March 29, 1966
      Princess Grace   June 19, 1965
*Oral History Project of the Herbert Hoover Presidential Library
Association Inc.*
      Kennedy, Rose Fitzgerald
Oral History Project of the Lyndon Baines Johnson Library
      Graham, Katharine   December 1970
      Humphrey, Hubert H.   July 11, 1974
      Onassis, Jacqueline Kennedy   January 11, 1974
Parmet, Herbert S., *Jack. The Struggles of John F. Kennedy*. The Dial
      Press, 1980.
Parmet, Herbert S., *JFK. The Presidency of John F. Kennedy*. The Dial
      Press, 1983.
Plimpton, George (editor), *American Journey, Interviews by Jean Stein*.
      Harcourt Brace Jovanovich, 1970.
Salinger, Pierre, *With Kennedy*. Doubleday, 1966.
Salinger, Pierre and Sander Vanocur (editors), *A Tribute to John F.
      Kennedy*. Encyclopaedia Britannica, 1964.
Schlesinger, Arthur M. Jr., *A Thousand Days*. Houghton Miffin Co., The
      Riverside Press, 1965.
Schlesinger, Arthur M. Jr., *Robert F. Kennedy and His Times*. Andre
      Deutsch Ltd, 1978.
Schulke, Flip (editor), *Martin Luther King*. W.W. Norton & Co., 1976.
Schwartz, Urs, *John F. Kennedy*. Paul Hamlyn, 1964.
Settel, T.S. (editor), *The Faith of JFK*. E.P. Dutton & Co., 1965.
Settel, T.S. (editor), *The Wisdom of JFK*. E.P. Dutton & Co., 1965.
Sorensen, Theodore C., *The Kennedy Legacy*. Macmillan 1969.
Sorensen, Theodore C., *Kennedy*. Harper & Row, 1965.
Thompson, Robert F. and Hortense Myers, *Robert F. Kennedy: The
      Brother Within*. Macmillan, David-Stewart
      Publishing Co., NY, 1962.
Toledano, Ralph de, *R.F.K. The Man who Would be President*. G.P.
      Putnam's Sons, 1967.
Turner, William N. and John G. Christian, *Assassination of Robert F.
      Kennedy*. Random House, 1978.
Van Rensselaer Thayer, Mary, *Jacqueline Bouvier Kennedy*. Doubleday,
      1961.
White, Theodore H., *The Making of the President 1960*. Atheneum,
      1961.
White, William S., *The Professional: Lyndon B. Johnson*. Houghton
      Mifflin Co., The Riverside Press, 1964.
Wills, Gary, *The Kennedy Imprisonment*. Atlantic, Little, Brown & Co.,
      1982.
Wyden, Peter, *Bay of Pigs*. Simon & Schuster, 1979.

INDEX

index continues overleaf

PHOTOGRAPHIC CREDITS

All photographs © Jacques Lowe except as noted below:

Courtesy the Kennedy Family and the John Fitzgerald Kennedy Library (pp.8, 9, 12, 14, 15, 17, 18, 20 to 31, 33, 34 below, 35 to 37, 40 below, 41, 44, 45, 46 to 50, 51 above, 56, 174, 175 above and below, 178 above, 183 to 185, 202, 203)

Courtesy the Lyndon Baines Johnson Library, Okamoto Photos (pp.242, 243 centre and right, 244 below, 247, 252 above)

Courtesy Holy Cross Archives (pp.10, 11, 13)

Marcus Adams (pp.42, 43)

© Bob Adelman (pp.177, 187, 244 above, 149, 254 above and below, 255 to 257)

Burton Berinsky (pp.246, 258, 259)

Black Star Photos
    (© Flip Schulke, p.176)
    (© Robert Lackenbach, pp.204, 205)
    (Michael Abramson, p.251 above)
    (Nacio Jan Brown, p.251 below)
    (Matt Heron, p.254 centre, pp.260, 261)
    (George Ballis, p.263 below)

Boston Globe (p.19)

Boston Herald (p.40 centre)

E.F. Foley (p.32)

Houghton Mifflin (Stephen Halport, p.16)

LIFE Magazine/Colorific
    (© Yale Joel, pp.52, 53)
    (© Lisa Larsen, p.55)
    (© Hank Walker, p.57)
    (© John Dominis, p.206)

London News Agency (p.38)

A.P. London (p.39)

Los Angeles Times Photo (Boris Yaro, p.266)

Magnum Photos
    (© Peter Hunter, p.40 above)
    (© Bob Henriques, p.156)
    (© Philip Jones Griffiths, pp.248, 250, 252 below, 253)
    (© Burt Glinn, pp.260, 261, 162, 163 above)
    (© Cornwell Capa, p.264)

Royal Atelier, NYC (p.34 above)

Woodfin Camp & Associates (©Dan Budnik, p.233)

Every effort has been made to locate the proprietors of the following material: Marcus Adams/Gilbert Adams (photograph pp.42/3); Bryn Mawr Publishers (Juno, *The Nude Frontier*); Aaron Payne ("I'll Remember"). If the proprietors will write to the publisher, formal arrangements will be made.

ACKNOWLEDGEMENTS

The author wishes to thank the many people who helped in the production of this book. Particular thanks are due to Stephen Smith, who encouraged the book and authorized the use of Kennedy family album photographs never before seen in book form, thereby greatly enhancing the early history in this book; to Alan Goodrich of the John Fitzgerald Kennedy Library, who gave countless hours of research to sometimes vague recollections of existing photographs and to Clay Felker, Joe Napolitan, David Powers and Pierre Salinger for reading the manuscript and commenting on it.

The author and publisher wish to thank the following for permission to quote from copyright material:

Alcatraz Corner Music Company Ltd/Chrysalis Music Ltd ("I Feel Like I'm Fixing to Die Rag"); Jonathan Cape Ltd on behalf of the estate of Robert Frost and Holt, Rinehart and Winston (poems from *The Poetry of Robert Frost* edited by Edward Connery Lathem, copyright 1923 © 1969 by Holt, Rinehart and Winston, copyright 1942, 1951 © 1961, 1962 by Robert Frost. Copyright © 1970 by Lesley Frost Ballantine); Chapple Music Ltd ("Camelot"); Collier Books, NY/Collier–Macmillan Ltd (*Vietnam Inc.* by Philip Jones Griffiths); William Collins and Sons and Company and Doubleday and Company (*Times to Remember* by Rose Fitzgerald Kennedy, copyright © 1974 by Joseph P. Kennedy Jr. Foundation); Joan Daves ("I Have a Dream" by Martin Luther King Jr., copyright © 1963 by Martin Luther King Jr., and "I've Been to the Mountaintop" by Martin Luther King Jr., copyright © 1968 Estate of Martin Luther King Jr.); EMI Music Ltd – Whitmark Music/Warner Bros. Music Inc. ("Sweet Adeline"); Erich Fried (translation of "Schulkinder" by Erich Fried); Harcourt Brace Jovanovich Inc. (*American Journey, The Times of Robert Kennedy, Interviews by Jean Stein* edited by George Plimpton, copyright © 1970 by Jean Stein van den Heuvel); Little Brown & Co. Inc. (*Khrushchev Remembers* with an introduction, commentary and notes by Edward Crankshaw, translated and edited by Strobe Talbott, copyright © 1970 by Little, Brown & Co. Inc.); Macmillan, London and Basingstoke (*At the End of the Day,* included in the six volumes of memoirs by Harold Macmillan); M.C.A. Music Ltd ("Eve of Destruction"); W.W. Norton and Company Inc. (*Thirteen Days, A Memoir of the Cuban Missile Crisis* by Robert F. Kennedy, copyright © 1971, 1969 by W.W. Norton and Company Inc. Copyright © 1968 by McCall Corporation); Regent Music Inc. ("Abraham, Martin and John"); The Society of Authors as the literary representative of the Estate of John Masefield ("John Fitzgerald Kennedy" by John Masefield); Ludlow Music Inc. Tro Essex Music Ltd ("We Shall Overcome").

For Jacques —

who was there
at the beginning —
and the last

with love

[signature]

Jan. 1963